T0381005

PARADIGM LOST

PARADIGM LOST

LEARNING AND LITERACY IN THE DIGITAL DIVIDE

Vicki J. Sapp

Algora Publishing
New York

Library of Congress Control Number: 2024947300

Names: Sapp, Vicki J., author.
Description:
From Google to ChatGPT, technology threatens to sweep students into
dependency and weakness in thinking and communicating. Prof. Vicki J.
Sapp helps educators, students, parents and the public to see the dangers and
recognize possible remedies, in the effort to keep education human centered and
strengthen it as the preserver of individual and cultural literacy—and freedom.

Cover artwork by Lilianne Leedy

Printed in the United States

Technologies change continuously. Media evolve. Networks emerge, die, expand, and contract. As Mary Hocks (2005) recently put it at a talk delivered at Michigan State University, one of the primary frustrations of researching digital rhetoric is that "technology is always already over." Disciplines, likewise, are living entities. Writing and other meaning-making practices certainly change shape due to the ebbs and flows of cultural events, historical happenings, economic shifts, and with the rise and adoption of information and communication technologies. This dynamic movement serves to remind us how powerful, potent, and important it is for us to analyze deeply the technological moment and the digital practices that emerge.

—DigiRhet.org

For what wears out the life of mortal men?
  'Tis that from change to change their being rolls;
'Tis that repeated shocks, again, again,
  Exhaust the energy of strongest souls.

—Matthew Arnold

TABLE OF CONTENTS

Preface: Apologia Pro Opus Suis

> We lead different lives when our experience of the
> world is mediated or interrupted.
>
> —Nate Anderson, *In Emergency, Break Glass: What
> Nietzsche Can Teach Us About Joyful Living in a Tech-
> Saturated World*

> To be everywhere is to be nowhere.
>
> —Seneca

In my half-century odyssey through education, from college days to quasi-retirement, I started with no internet, just paper textbooks and a Royal typewriter, and ended up moving mostly online for teaching, doing research and writing. I've gotten a lot of experience in these four decades. As I transitioned over time, from textbook to TikTok and blackboard to Blackboard, through all the learning-support media, I did indeed learn a lot. There were even victorious moments; about ten years ago, when a colleague whom I had revered for her celebrity-status scholarship learned that I had started teaching online, she said, "Wow, you must know a lot about computers. I'm afraid I'm still a novice in that world." She had compared us, and I had come out on top, at least in terms of medium if not message.

More than a decade before, about the mid-1990s, the phrase "digital divide" had come on the scene. Apparently there was one of these between my colleague and me, which made me a little proud as I had thought of myself as a novice in that world. There are stages, if not a continuum, of achievement along the divide, and one feels like this has an open end, as one will always be competitive while the skill horizon retreats into the technology-dominated future. One of my students even posted a Facebook feed with an informative blurb and many comments about all of the "Gens": IGen, GenZ, Millennials, GenX, Boomers, and the earlier 20th-century predecessors called "The Silent Generation." While these last were hardly silent in terms of action and achievement, I assume the adjective derives from their inability to have continuously blared their existences electronically across creation. In fact, on Facebook I frequently see postings not only from fellow Boomers but also from later Gens, looking back longingly to the Silent times. The thesis of my student's posting seemed to be that all these Gens are defined by their position along the Digital Divide in the temporal sense I am using here as my main focus. One starts to believe that everyone born after 1950 must be first identified in terms of their relationship with and use of information technology.

The phrase "digital divide" started as, and has dominated as, an economic indicator: those who could financially afford access to high-tech devices and access, and those who couldn't. Later, it would also include those who wouldn't, that is, who refused the new charge to go digital. My colleague was a wouldn't; she could well afford the priciest access; she just hadn't found this wide and steep learning curve important enough to occupy her time. Nowadays, such an attitude is more than inconvenient. One must not only become an ongoing apprentice in the ever-rapidly changing techno workshop; one must also have a "social media presence." In how-tos about marketing your book, "having significant social media outreach" seems a significant requirement. I see that my professional credentials somewhat mitigate the fact that I stay off of social media, with the exception of Facebook, which was forced upon me by students who insisted a decade ago that any good professional must be social-media connected. But I stay off it except to post education articles, because these days one misguided word can get you canceled in education. And writers know that misguided words often slip out innocently enough. In fact, if I posted an article defending the old print-canon ways, I might get canceled.

So, what are these old print-canon ways, and how do they compare and contrast with the new digital ways? How different are these two ways, aka literacies? What drives and characterizes their differences?

Print literacy is generally conceived of as a passive, linear, slow, isolated, detached monomodal process. (I borrow these modifiers and those below for digital, recalling them from current memory, from a lot of sources consulted over the crossing.) The reader's perception is generally confined to following and interpreting the verbal strings on the page. By contrast, digital literacy is seen as active, nonlinear, fast, communal, multimodal, and requiring multiple perceptual if not intellectual processes: not only verbal but also visual, audial, and even kinesthetic as the reader must navigate multiple sites and links, punching keys and scrolling. Note even in this typical diction of comparison, the invidious situating of print and digital modes. Print seems almost like a punishment, by solitary confinement and ensuing boredom. Those who stress this difference rarely explore the positives of print-literate qualities: time, depth, autonomy, deliberation, reflection. Digital literacy is seen almost universally as literacy progress promising smarter, better, more inclusive learning.

In her study "What's the Hype? E-Books Take Over Education," Southern New Hampshire University student Lilianne Leedy echoes one side of the issue as she argues that online reading is inferior to print reading in terms of online's potential for distraction, compromised retention, and relative diffi-culty of access. Leedy, a 21-year-old college student here in 2024, confesses her own preference for print and her practice of working with printed paper copies of class reading materials. She explains her concern:

> I am a parent and step-parent myself, and I have noticed a profound impact technology has had on the comprehension/retention of informa-tion on my stepson. After speaking with many other parents regarding this issue, it's a shared concern. I graduated high school before the pandemic, in which e-books were not used within the classroom like they are now. I attended college virtually in 2020, and I noticed a remarkable difference in my ability to comprehend and retain the information presented in a digital format. I began to print out all the things I needed to read, as the e-material was too distracting (1).

It is commonly believed that students prefer online reading; however, in Leedy's experience and as I have observed in my practice, this is not neces-sarily true. E-texts win out for them because they "aren't heavy and cumber-some and don't hurt my back"—medium over message—and also for their ease of accessibility anywhere and everywhere, a key attraction of all things cyber. Accessible, that is, if the student has access to the tech and Wi-Fi—and both are up and functioning when needed. "The internet was down" is, next to unfortunate situations with relatives, their most common excuse for unsubmitted work.

Amanda Abrams, in her article "An Education in Scrolling," addresses a challenge familiar to any educator paying attention in a tech-bound class-room: how to keep students on task when they're on screen? "This, it seems, is public school in the post-COVID era," Abrams reports as she describes how the transition to screen-based education, required by the pandemic, has persisted and intensified, eroding the quality of the classroom experience. Clarifying that she is not complaining about the media themselves, educational software, and learning platforms such as Canvas, she insists: "And I'm absolutely not blaming teachers, whom I've found to be almost universally devoted to students' growth, even under increasingly dismal conditions; they can't be expected to monitor 20-plus kids' screens" (4). Those "increasingly dismal conditions" have largely to do, both during class lessons and in the larger picture of students' 24/7 addiction to screen life, with the infinite allure, access, and distractibility of screens. Abrams' article, buried inside a local progressive weekly paper, spotlights the rising tide of parental concern, such as Leedy's described above, for education moved onscreen where kids "invariably get distracted and fall into an internet rabbit hole" (5). Yet, the solution of the mentors so far has seemed to be abandonment of paper and book and capitulation to the screen along with its new challenges and pitfalls.

The clearest analysis of print-digital difference I have found is a 2011 study by J. Rowsell and Maureen Walsh, who offer a breakdown (qtd. directly below) of different pathways and angles of difference as they propose that digital literacy involves the following "more" and "less" than print:

- More work in other contexts such as homes and communities (Gonzales, Moll, & Amanti, 2005)
- Less emphasis on cognitive development (Gee, 1996) as in what happens in our brains or minds and more emphasis on cultural practices
- More research examining the interface between identity and libteracy development (Gee, 1996; 1999)
- Less of a divide between oral and written cultures (Ong, 1982)
- An acknowledgment of the screen as our dominant text structure (Cope & Kalantzis, 2000; Kress, 2003)
- An expansion of definitions from print logic, reading and writing, to screen logic, designing, redesigning, remixing (Cope & Kalantzis, 2000)

Note the basic claim or "acknowledgment" that screens are our dominant "text." I find it interesting because I have always thought of screens as a delivery tool for reading, one that can offer essays, articles, stories, poems, chapters, novels, and all verbal efforts along with the ever-expanding types of visual ones, both static and video. In this very acknowledgment, we see that the message has indeed become this dominant medium whose ever-complexifying learning curve and requirements for nimble navigation skills become an integral component of the literacy—a demanding level of investment relatively absent in the written page or photographic image.

Rowsell and Walsh report, "Multi-literacies scholars claim that the screen governs our understanding of the world and curricula needs [sic] to reflect this dramatic shift in our ideological and interpretative frame." Because screens are literally in everyone's hands these days, the medium has restructured not only our lifestyles but also the ways we know and believe. Moreover, education must bow to this dominance, as also happened gradually with the printed medium, over centuries after the printing press and the book's rise to popular consumption. However, as I will argue throughout here, the screen mode's speed, saturation, relentless innovation, and challenge (by sheer diversity and volume) to authority—even truth as possible or desirable—make it very different from the paradigm shift brought about by the print medium. Of course, we must always learn new media, and these media are always tied in to power structures and cultural dominance. But where the printed book's underlying power structures have been confined to the traditional layers dictated by education, profession, money, and other familiar stratifications—the digital power structures can be seen as belonging to everyone, everywhere, at once. (We might even think of digital texts as literary cryptocurrency.) If the print medium can be viewed as based on invidious distinction and contingent authority—the digital can be thought to neutralize the very concept of authority.

New-media digital scholars claim that their medium expands and democratizes literacy across nations, cultures, ethnicities, and languages in ways less possible or impossible for the print medium. Has this made for a pretty paradigm shift so far? In some ways, yes, as we can connect with each other and so much information freely, 24/7 around the globe. This is thought to be an unquestionable boon, especially to parents with kids studying abroad, say, such as your writer here who fairly worships WhatsApp for keeping her connected and reassured with world-traveler offspring. But let's look at the other side: a continuous rise in violence, suicide, anxiety, depression, isolation—not to mention attention challenges, societal degradation, and even obesity and other physical health problems. (For the most recent blockbuster on this collateral damage, see Jonathan Haidt's 2024 *The Anxious Generation*.) In education, in the U.S., everyone laments the "crisis" allegedly brought about by the COVID pandemic isolation but well known by us in the business to have been perceptible for years in our students' skill degradation, to the point where an ever-expanding majority are not prepared for college work. Cheating—catapulted to new heights and modes with AI—is the new normal.

My arguments throughout here are grounded in our academic culture's invidious distinction between print and digital literacy, in my view the most significant "divide" we need to consider. Higher education, at least today, is aligning its policies, goals, and methodologies with digital dominance while retaining, necessarily, the bulk of its practice in print-literate-based curriculum—if not paper books, at least the brand of literacy reflected in their use. (I speak only for the liberal arts here, which are under attack on this and other fronts, political and cultural.) This is causing great stress in the classroom, as suggested by Leedy in chorus with a great many others. This stress also signals the tremendous opportunity for learning and growth, on both sides of the podium, and this is a plus for us all. However, I want to remind that we are still "between," and I write first of all to those out there who are feeling and suffering from this stress and who might have even quit teaching from premature burnout. I propose that for many, such burnout has come from not only the great new digital learning time, effort, and learning-culture impositions, along with adverse changes in our culture and students' attitudes and behaviors—but that these latter themselves derive in large part from the downside of digital culture.

The phrase "digital divide" featured in my title is intended to represent the "wandering between two worlds" notion I have borrowed from Matthew Arnold, the 19th-century poet who lamented, in his *Stanzas from the Grand Chartreuse*, his own fate to wander forlornly between the two worlds of faith and science, nature and artifice, pastoral and industrial values. Longing for the spiritual and intellectual wealth of the old world, the poet recalls:

> For rigorous teachers seized my youth,
> And purged its faith, and trimm'd its fire,
> Show'd me the high, white star of Truth,
> There bade me gaze, and there aspire.
> Even now their whispers pierce the gloom:
> What dost thou in this living tomb?

This describes all too well the way this old professor, educated by older professors in the days before the techno-takeover, feels. How do their Truths fare, and how can they help me and my students in the depthless, affect-less virtual tomb? Nowadays, these teachers would be censured for their sage-on-the-stage pretensions to authority over the pupil. To the digital divide definition, I will add to the "can't" and "won't" a third—"shouldn't." Crossing the divide between print and digital literacies, some of us might feel that we have not only lost something valuable from our old "rigorous teachers" in the warm print world of classroom and textbook (and Royal typewriter, which I can still see, smell, and feel beneath my searching fingers)—we have also added something dangerous and overwhelming. But to this "shouldn't," I need to add a meta-shouldn't: what humble servant of education today dares bring up a notion like this? Powerful experts in the business—Mark Bauerlein, Sherry Turkle, Nicholas Carr, Jean Twenge, and many others—have dared to do so. Feeling as I have about the gradual and victorious cyber-invasion over the past four decades of my temple, I have had a lot of things to say as well.

The following discussion shares many of these thoughts with you, here, after I have finally figured out how to air my own "shouldn't," I hope in a way that doesn't bring down too much censure if not cancellation. I suppose that if this is now in your hands, I can no longer avoid this censure since a successful piece of writing must of necessity go out on social media, and out there you can post that puppies and kittens are adorable and bring down a hail of censure. I'm sure that you can by now find me on Instagram, which my students have all assured me I would love. (One especially recommended Reddit for me, and I'm not sure how to take that.) I can guarantee you that even if I loved it, I would still distrust and fear it. This distrust and fear are not unlike the anti-vaxxers' today—those anti-tech conspiracy theorist dinosaurs who must also be ignorant, paranoid, or just plain lazy!

My own career as an educator for over four decades reflects the time between no internet and pretty much all internet. It is a narrative of gradual discovery, with some shocking irruptions, within the major paradigm shift underway; how exciting and wearying to live through its course so far! There are those who insist that this one is not really different from the last millennium's paradigm shifts from no books for anyone to books for scholars only, to books available to the general population. I could not disagree more. Looking back, I now see what a tremendous impact this most recent shift has had (and so fast), is still having, and will increasingly have on my field in the future. I have had the opportunity to learn a great deal—but it has left me tired and sad.

I recently had a conversation with a forty-something colleague who imagines herself "old" because she visited a younger colleague's class and saw the latter's comparatively superior agility with new online tools. "We just didn't learn all this when I was in grad school." I didn't either, I thought, too cumbersome with stone tablets. (eye-roll emoji) "Did it make for better teaching?" I asked. "Oh yes, at least it must have." Why this "must have"? "Because we have to go where the students are," she sighed. How many times have I heard this trite bit, ridiculous to someone who studied when this notion would have made no sense to anyone? As much as we loved *All My Children* on our student union TV back in my college days, to suggest that we must run college classes like soap operas would have been laughable. There were no screens in our dorms, in our rooms, on our desks, in our hands. We learned well enough, too. But as we would soon realize, heralded by Marshall McLuhan's new-media theories grounded in television, the medium does indeed pack a powerful and even dominant message. We have learned that the medium can come to dominate the message and render it superfluous and even powerless. We are learning that the medium now controls education in deeper, more comprehensive, and aggressive ways than the book could do.

There is one sort of consoling possibility for the weary wanderer. I have re-thought one more definition of the digital divide as a generational rift between the so-called digital immigrant and digital native. As a devotee of both McLuhan and Neil Postman, who wrote their stirring critiques about television in the mid-twentieth century, I am inclined to believe that the Boomer and the IGen-er are not so far apart: both became and are addicted to screens. There is an emblematic photo of one-year-old me, in 1954, pulling myself upright by embracing the wooden cabinet of our black-and-white TV, pressing my baby cheek to its cold dark screen. I-Gen-ers and I share a passion for the medium of the screen. (And to think—I can now receive my childhood-weekly twenty-minute infusion of *I Love Lucy* in a continuous episode stream, "binge-watching," and on my phone, anywhere, anytime.) The very significant difference is that at my students' age, I had access to my TV screen for maybe a couple of hours a day, if that, watching with family evenings in my parents' living room, what they wanted to watch, whereas today, we all have it for ourselves 24/7 anywhere and everywhere. Way too many of my students have confessed to sleeping with their phone under the pillow, texting and surfing on it all night. An astonishing number of my geriatric friends report similar addictive habits. Experts studying this have told us how destructive sleep deprivation is to the brain. And sleep deprivation is just a start to the many ways technology has compromised our health, physical and mental.

Some Generic Considerations

Here follows a history of how I got to this study. It includes scholarship, literary criticism, narrative nonfiction, personal essays, fits of ranting, and even a bit of fiction. It might even appear to some as the scattershot musings of an internet multitasker, and they wouldn't be far off. But it all reflects my decades of wandering through the digital divide as a consumer and practitioner of education in its various avatars, sustained by the rigorous teachings of my past and aimed, however doubtfully and regretfully, toward the electronic promise of the future. Even if that promise is from Satan (see Chapter One here), it deserves our attention and critique.

This volume has had many predecessor efforts, including a desperate outcry from a dozen years ago, a presentation prepared for an English conference. This sad PowerPoint, a lone voice in the woods, was, against its author's more honest inclinations, entitled "Understanding Mediacy." (I neither wished to understand it nor thought I could.) I had come up with this portmanteau, "Mediacy," from "media" and "literacy"; it reflected my growing awareness that my students and I were increasingly sitting in two different classrooms: print and digital literacies. While I was, as their instructor, superabundantly equipped to train them in the old ways of print literacy, I was struggling for purchase on the perimeters of the new digital economy. My struggle was compounded by the fact that, echoing Matthew Arnold, print literacy was hardly "dead," and digital literacy was hardly "powerless to be born" as it was, literally, in our face almost 24/7—Big Brother's screen that we had voluntarily and joyfully welcomed a couple of decades before. This takeover of our attention, thought, and emotion would continue, very fast, to broaden, deepen, and strengthen its hold on us—and will continue to, even faster and without remedy.

With this initial foray into the public judgment sphere of a professional conference, I was not sure what I hoped to accomplish. I do not recall any reaction to my presentation from anyone at the conference; the only reaction I had was from my own department chair who, as the lone colleague attending my prior practice run on campus, whispered to me, "You've got something there," almost as if I was revealing something secret. You see, I was becoming painfully aware that a gap had opened between me and my students, a relationship that had been for decades a bonded, happy collusion in the pursuit of advanced and enhanced literacy, transacted on paper and together in campus spaces. We still did read books and articles, and we still did meet on campus for classes; however, the vibe had decidedly changed. Increasingly, I came across admonitions that "you must go where your students are." This meant, without question, the internet, and it would require a whole lot of extra work for us already hyper-extended instructors of a half-dozen each, per term, Freshman Composition classes.

In spite of increasing fatigue and suspicion, my efforts to "understand mediacy" and to "go where my students were" persisted for their sake, as it was my job to teach and guide them. I created more techno-dystopian PowerPoints for more conferences. After one especially impassioned analysis of mine regarding the rigors of defining, understanding, and blundering through the "digital divide," a colleague stood up and, likely representing the sentiments of at least half the audience, demanded to know of me, "What's your point?"

My point, at least in part, was to warn us educators that one day, sooner than we might realize, we would become obsolete. As Bill Joy reports in his "Why the Future Doesn't Need Us," "Ray [Kurzweil] said, simply, that the changes would come gradually, and that we would get used to them" (296). Joy's title and Kurzweil's belief both speak compellingly to educators, who have already been demoted from "sage on the stage" to "guide on the side," mere "facilitators" of learning, and might soon slip entirely, along with brick-and-mortar institutions and physical classrooms, into archaism if not nonexistence. (For more coverage of this, see Chapter 3 of my study here, "The Divide Conquers.") This devolution, awareness of which has been supported so far by our experience with the COVID-19 pandemic and dependence on online education, might well be fueled by financial reasons: the physical is more expensive than the virtual, at least to the institution, after all. Joy, speaking of technological change in general, contextualizes, "We are aggressively pursuing the promises of these new technologies within the now-unchallenged system of global capitalism and its manifold financial incentives and competitive pressures." While he does not mention education in his essay, again, his point is spot-on for my argument here throughout.

But speaking of archaism, back to the early 'aughts and my initial zeal to come to understand my new master, so I could do its bidding even as my sense and sensibility recoiled. There is a great meme out there showing a pharaoh-like, whip-wielding character standing over a cowering person. The latter says, "I don't like this system," and the former responds, "Well, then, why do you stay?" Such is the irony of any protest such as mine today, a concern shared by many as evidenced by all the social media attention to Aldous Huxley's *Brave New World* prophecy, "People will come to love their oppression, to adore the technologies that undo their capacities to think."

In my conference-hopping, I switched from PowerPoint rants to the essay, a cooler approach. In this volume, you will find the puffed-up title, "A Humanist Educator from the Digital Divide." Humanists, with one sensible shoe permanently grounded in the 19th century, puff themselves up to appear bigger before the oncoming foe. They cling to outmoded notions such as the value of "RL"—real life, with thoughts and feelings connected to biological bodies and public, in-person social experiences.

Thoughts, feelings, and bodies are limited and vulnerable. The internet is infinite and unconquerable (until someone "pulls the plug," that is, and more on this obvious vulnerability later). Along my way, I had come to realize that I had no way to stand up for the old ways via scholarship. Many have tried, many have written very interesting books and articles on, if not the defense of print literacy, at least the questioning of its digital conqueror's motives and goals. I began to think that my strongest voice might just come from the experience itself, of "wandering between two wor(l)ds" dying and newborn, print and digital. After all, this new paradigm shift had not happened and was not happening overnight and could not be neatly categorized and packaged into good and bad, old/useless and new/useful pedagogy. It all was just happening, and continuously changing, and so fast.

As recently as late 2022, I received this message from a colleague:

Hi everyone,

In case you wanted to play around with media literacy in your courses and assign work centered on podcasts, memes, cartoons, and so on, an expert from UCLA is holding a 5-part virtual series of media assignments you can implement into your courses.

Now, this department—in spite of a dedicated faculty and fine curriculum—suffers an abysmal pass rate, less than 50%, for its freshman English courses. There is, of course, a complexity of reasons for this, including the historical ones of poverty, poor K-12 preparation, and lives fraught with all sorts of responsibilities. However, I'd like to put as #1 our students' media addictions and the surprising apparent department view that media-literacy instruction can still be classified as "playing around" by those who "want" to, "and so on." What's the point? The point is just that, as another conference colleague wailed, illustratively brandishing her phone like a grenade, "THEY HAVE BEATEN US." Her point? She simply could not get her students off their phones long enough to learn much, with the correlative observation that "they won't read anything and have become terribly lazy, rude, and disrespectful." This was not at an average American institution but rather a highbrow foreign university. She was joined in her wailing by some fellow American top-tier colleagues who claimed that three-fourths of their own privileged, well-prepared students admitted to continuous plagiarism, with the bespoke assistance of the internet. One of my students recently and confidently informed me that "80% of your classes are now using ChatGPT to write their assignments." Of the 20% who presumably don't, how many of these genuinely want to learn—and how many still just don't know about Chat? As my snitch demanded, "What's the problem? You ask for a paper—you get a paper." Oh, silly me, expecting students in an increasingly consumer-business-modeled academic economy to focus on something other than the commodity!

What's my point? My point is that we educators seem to be screwed, at least by our traditional standards. Students are being robbed. We all are being robbe. If you want to take a population down, I can think of no better start than the massive betrayal of undoing our students' capacities to think.

As much as you'd like to speak the direct truth, you simply cannot entitle your study of the transition from print to digital paradigm *The Internet Has Screwed Us*. After all, it's just another paradigm shift; the internet has brought us so much good; the author is just a dinosaur digitally divided from the brave new world, "and so on." Adam Gopnik, in his 2011 "The Information: How the Internet Gets Inside Us," helpfully proposes three categories of shift questioners: "the Never-Betters, the Better-Nevers, and the Ever-Wasers." These labels are concisely self-explanatory, but they merit some commentary. The Never-Betters love all the new technology, the Better-Nevers (aka Luddites) think it all should just go away, and the Ever-Wasers point out, not inaccurately, that change is always the norm.

All of these positions have merit, but there is an argument so powerful that it really doesn't need these others: IT HAS BEATEN US; it's not going away, and the future will be largely transacted virtually, on all fronts, for reasons to be posited throughout this volume. The Never-Betters blind themselves to collateral damage. The Better-Nevers are left behind to weep over their quill and scroll. The Ever-Wasers just go about their business, whatever. Must we settle the case and declare it useless to study, analyze, and criticize the phenomenon? Any educator worth their salt would yell a resounding "no," because that's what we do—poke at and talk about things. Since my career started forty years ago, I have been driven by, many would say obsessed with, the goals, purposes, and strategies of education. I have always kept the closest eye on meta-pedagogy, arguably to the detriment of my pedagogy, or at least its content. By meta-pedagogy, I mean obsessively ruminating over the impact of the subject text and medium on my students' learning and lives. Having taught over forty different English courses and in multiple departments; having run programs from "developmental" to "honors"; having conference-trotted for decades; but mostly having gotten to know tens of thousands of students quite well and observed and listened to their challenges—I figure I at least have some ethos in this game. As we rhetoricians know, ethos comes with its partners, logos (facts) and pathos (appeal to feelings).

I dare compare my efforts here to those of the greats who have already devoted themselves to writing books on my topic (I reference these critics—Haidt, Postman, Bauerlein, Carr, Turkle, Twenge, Skrbina, and others throughout). However, mine features more pathos (emotion), and academia has traditionally disliked pathos, reflecting our culture's general bias against the emotional in argument. Consequently, my logos is scattered everywhere and sniffs for danger, continuously, and for evidence supporting my argument: we are screwed. So finding my genre has been fraught with anxiety, challenge, confusion, and doubt.

As I was mapping out my chapters here—scholarly investigations, personal narratives, literature reviews, creative nonfictions, short fictions, and more—I attempted to find a unifying generic link: how to frame all of these diverse experiences as an educator? Then one afternoon, as I was driving along listening to NPR, on that old legacy medium of radio, the answer came to me. I stumbled across an interview with Margot Jefferson about her new book, *Constructing a Nervous System*. Defending her choice of weighing memoir over scholarship, she observed that memoir is equated with vulnerability, while scholarship or "criticism" is equated with power. What she asserted, though, is that "Vulnerability can be critical power." She had realized that she could write from her "lacks," and she had learned to "assess your lacks to see how they might be useful to you" (NPR interview, A1, 7/21/22).

So, still feeling the sting of my lacks in my print-grounded understanding of what to do in a new digital age, I realized, from hearing Ms. Jefferson's own experience, that I could use my vulnerability. I could share my decades-long experience wandering between two worlds in a major paradigm shift while trying my hardest to be there for my students and help them advance themselves through their education. This also amounts to a wandering between two words, as we hopefully seek commonalities and exhaustedly confront differences between "print" and "digital" literacies—all the while wondering how to wrangle our experience into constructive pedagogy. You see, in spite of popular pronouncement, we in higher education still depend heavily on print literacy values. And, in spite of our deeply entrenched values, we must rally to create constructive and possibly brand-new curriculum for a digital age. This is nothing new for educators; however, I argue here that this has become so much more difficult for educators already laboring under our time's other major challenges of outsize classes, low pay, poor support, changing (for the worse) socioeconomic conditions for their students, violent crime and too much more. Our exhaustion before socioeconomic affronts becomes increasingly compounded by our need to go digital; and while this requires little investment from the casual internet surfer—getting good at it means everything to the responsible educator charged to keep teaching effectively. When you load up an absurdly underpaid part-time instructor with thirty composition students in four or five sections, and the continuous requirement to find these students where they are, online, and feed them what they are used to, negotiating the technology that adds an extra time and labor burden to normal class prep and activity—an extra commitment colleagues have estimated to be at least 30%—well, there you oscillate between lamentations and lessons.

What is happening to us now, as we "wander"? How are we feeling? How are we doing? The lessons are, I believe from long experience, lamentable, elusive, and not infrequently disheartening. I will defer here to the classic mentor of any of us concerned about the paradigm shift in education between the two worlds. Consider the 1960s perspective of Marshall McLuhan from his *Understanding Media*:

> In the past, the effects of media were experienced more gradually, allowing the individual and society to absorb and cushion their impact to some degree. Today, in the electronic age of instantaneous communication, I believe that our survival, and at the very least our comfort and happiness, is predicated on understanding the nature of our new environment, because unlike previous environmental changes, the electric media constitute a total and near-instantaneous transformation of culture, values, and attitudes. This upheaval generates great pain and identity loss, which can be ameliorated only through a conscious awareness of its dynamics. If we understand the revolutionary transformations caused by new media, we can anticipate and control them; but if we continue in our self-induced subliminal trance, we will be their slaves. (Playboy 5).

In this volume I speak, joining other noteworthy voices in the wilderness, from our "subliminal trance," and if having any constructive purpose, I call for us to understand. Even if you yourself are a digital native—that is, having held a smartphone since birth—you still must transact the business of the classroom's public space. As we will consider here, our human transactions and public spaces seem to have turned so complicated and imperiled. From this, I am reaching out to colleagues, students, and anyone concerned about education and more—our shared physical and digital spaces, our humanity. Who would be excluded from this?

I choose (read: am forced) to feel some optimism—not because I actually do feel it (I'm too big a fan of dystopian and apocalyptic thinking) but rather because, in four decades of teaching, I have come to realize that optimism is our only choice as educators. Our students had no fault or choice to bring us where we are, and our task is to help them where they are. Of course, there are optimistic and constructive pathways into digital literacy, and learning and practicing them is exciting, fulfilling our chosen destinies as educators:

to adapt, to learn to apply what we know to where they are, and to let the old guide and support the new.

"Isn't it pretty to think so?" sighed Hemingway. Even if you've read through all this, hopeless and remaining so, that's fine, too. As Mephistoph-eles quipped to Doctor Faustus, who asked, "Why does Lucifer want my soul?" *Solamen miseris socios habuisse doloris.* Misery loves company. So take my textual hand and follow me into—if not the hell, at least the Purgatory—of paradigm shift where we must suffer, struggle, and learn.

Introduction: A Herstory of the Argument

> Everything that deceives can be said to enchant.
>
> —Plato

Far too frequently—as if there were any frequency at which one could tolerate such things—I have reeled from the "breaking news" of yet another mass shooting. An 18-year-old identifying with white supremacy journeyed far from his home to a supermarket, where he shot a number of people, killing at least ten. He wore on his forehead a camera, so he could broadcast the event on social media. So once more, the hand-wringing, along with "thoughts and prayers," about guns, mental illness, hate crimes, and other obvious current societal plagues. The camera and the broadcast did get a mention.

Demanding my close attention was a *New York Times* Opinion essay entitled "My College Kids Are Not OK" (May 13, 2022). I welcomed this title because it boldly said what I have known and bewailed for a long time now. The usual prime suspect is, of course, the aftershocks of the pandemic with the moving of classes online. In the comments section, commenters blamed everything else from George Bush to parents, teachers, standardized testing, I could go on...and a few pointed to screen life as the consuming distraction it is.

What links these two tragic scenarios is, without question, the internet. I would naturally believe such a thing as the original title of this meditation was *The Internet Has Screwed Us*. (A better grammatical choice would be, *We Have Screwed Ourselves with the Internet*.) Wise friends with cooler heads contraindicated this title as "too extreme/radical/monocular" and just "untrue." I agree with them, yet I am sticking with my judgment. The two positions are not mutually exclusive; in fact, their contradiction is one of the most powerful and fascinating phenomena, possibly of history or at least of my own observation. The internet owns us, it serves us; and we serve it, and we love it; and it is destroying us, at least as we have long under-stood ourselves, our purpose, and modus operandi as human (or at least as humanist educators). Back to the two tragic scenarios: both the not-OK college kids and, more horrifically, the serial killer are victims of the internet. They have unfolded the latter's downfall through internet dark-web white supremacy sites. And as for the former, these have been amused, distracted, and deceived by the internet, in both society and school, to the point where they have lost the connection and salvation of actual learning, not to mention the nurturing community of their fellows.

Anyone attracted to this line of thinking can do no better than start with Neil Postman, media and culture philosopher and prophet, who in his *Amusing Ourselves to Death* (the title says everything) warned us as far back as 1985:

> What Orwell feared were those who would ban books. What Huxley feared was that there would be no reason to ban a book, for there would be no one who wanted to read one. Orwell feared those who would deprive us of information. Huxley feared those who would give us so much that we would be reduced to passivity and egoism. Orwell feared that the truth would be concealed from us. Huxley feared the truth would be drowned in a sea of irrelevance. Orwell feared we would become a captive culture. Huxley feared we would become a trivial culture.... As Huxley remarked in *Brave New World Revisited*, the civil libertarians and rationalists who are ever on the alert to oppose tyranny 'failed to take into account man's almost infinite appetite for distractions.' In 1984, Huxley added, people are controlled by inflicting pain. In *Brave New World*, they are controlled by inflicting pleasure. In short, Orwell feared that what we hate will ruin us. Huxley feared that what we love will ruin us. (xix–xx)

Today, as we are distracted by constant reports of political chaos, violent crime, the pain inflicted by wars and conflicts in this eternally violent world, and the war on women's bodily autonomy and freedom, the street drugs killing so many, which are all truly enemies in the normal sense—we will do well to keep in mind the enemy that loves us, and we love it. Tyrants, patriarchal oppressors, serial killers, and murderous poisons have been with us always, and we try our best to run from these. But today, this new enemy that loves us and owns us seduces and uses us, its victims, as its enthralled weapon of mass (self-) destruction. This enemy's size, speed, saturation, and scorn for any standards of judgment, much less truth, might just allow it to be the end of us humans. I say this because from my viewpoint of seven decades, with print values shot into my blood and bones, I have come to imagine the gradual impending end, at the hands of the new digital gods, of pretty much everything I have held sacred: local community, family, peace, learning, thinking—and now, with AI, humanity.

But as my wise friends advise, this radical position is, if not untrue, at least so all-encompassing as to make it questionable, for anyone capable of critical thinking, as any kind of useful intellectual pathway or certainly any book anyone would care to read. Plus, apocalypse is depressing and exhausting. I have generally preferred dystopia, and the difference between the two is this: in apocalypse, you're hopelessly screwed, and all you can do is scramble to survive until it is no longer possible to do so. But with dystopia, there is hope and worthiness in the struggle to amend the wrong.

I will choose dystopia, not because I actually believe that we can hope to save ourselves from our demon lover—but because I am an educator, and we are by trade familiar with an ongoing and impossible but nonetheless affirming struggle against ignorance and hopelessness. Education also gives me a focus for my study, one where I have great experience and for which I have great respect. So the stakes are high for me to work myself out of despair, at least long enough to tell the truth about what the internet has done, in the long traditions of my world, to education and learning itself.

Do not worry, this is most certainly not to be, at least not entirely, a bitter rant against technology and certainly not against students. Because, you see, I have always respected my students and enjoyed joyful, mind-and-soul-sustaining work with them. I have reason to believe they have felt the same about me. (If you don't believe me, check out my Rate My Professor sites; RMP represents one of the tracks of internet evil for education, but it does have its uses.) No, I write this not to bury my students but to praise them, at least for their perseverance in our war against them. With the exception of the student-loan crisis (an evil surpassing even the capability of the mythic Satan), this is a passive war, born of inattention, fear, and capitulation. I refer to Mark Bauerlein's *The Dumbest Generation* (2008), a pioneer effort to map and analyze the lost ability, due to the internet and social media, of our young Americans to function effectively not only in academia but also in the social and professional adult world. I myself have interpreted Bauerlein's provocative title differently than his argument might first suggest: I believe that he ultimately reveals the adults in these young folks' lives—their parents, teachers, school administrators, etc.—as the true "dumbest genera-tion" who failed to recognize the damage inflicted by unrestricted access to screens, misguided ideas of youth's capacity for self-direction, and helpless-ness before the addictive new medium. He calls this, concisely and aptly, "the betrayal of the mentors." Think of this study in your hands as an analysis of the mentors' betrayal. I pray that we mentors can amend our ways, but I cannot imagine how, given that all Bauerlein's critiques still hold—and tech-nology's overtaking of education and our society has advanced much in the past sixteen years and proceeds at warp speed. But since I have always had faith in youth and my colleagues, and education is my religion that is founda-tional to that faith, I push on. We owe them and it, if not a way out, at least an accompanied and a critical pathway within.

The mentors cannot and should not turn over all the cyber-temple tables. I must say I have also loved the internet, especially as an educator and a writer. What person who has devoted their life and career to the pursuit of learning can entirely hate that which brings all that information, good and bad, before their eyes at the mere touch of a button? Especially when that person started their academic career in the dank bowels of brick-and-mortar libraries, in "the stacks," clawing for hours, paranoid and sneezing, through musty shelves for information? Plus, you cannot beat the immediate fact and source-checking capabilities of online writing. Having typed my 250-page doctoral thesis on a typewriter, I know well how much time and energy word processing technology and the internet at one's fingertips saves for the sake of one's actual thinking and writing. The increase in time and energy efficiency is nothing short of phenomenal. And what does technology bring us, if not perfect efficiency, or at least its potential? If we can just get our entire education system online and under surveillance, everyone can learn everything and do it much faster!

Your author here sets out to interrogate such ideas and propose that not only are they irrational and dangerous, but also they are sent by Satan to ruin us—see the next chapter here. Surely this is beyond the pale. But she will speak her truth. So put this book down now if you're so skeptical or offended that you cannot carry on. Aside from some experts like Bauerlein who dare to report their well-researched and closely observed truths, those who dare to attack or even question the internet's value to education run the risk of being thought a Luddite, lazy, or just plain crazy. Even when their own experience of the damage done in their classrooms, or from their child's learning experience, or on the news informs them that something is very wrong here, the addiction and brainwashing are just too strong. This author doesn't have much faith in a revolutionary outcome from such conversations, including the one underway here, anyway.

> S'io credesse che mia risposta fosse
> A persona che mai tornasse al mondo,
> Questa fiamma staria senza piu scosse.
> Ma percioche giammai di questo fondo
> Non torno vivo alcun, s'i'odo il vero,
> Senza tema d'infamia ti rispondo.

I borrow the Dantean epigraph (*Inferno*, Canto 27) from T.S. Eliot's "The Love Song of J. Alfred Prufrock." Prufrock, believing that neither he nor his readers can ever escape the hell of self-doubt and self-loathing in modern society, feels liberated to tell the truth to his fellow captives about his experience. I know that no one reading this can escape technopoly (Postman's term), unless by quitting school and their jobs and living in a cave in the remote woods—impractical and undesirable non-solutions. Recall Samuel Johnson's *Rasselas*, where the Hermit tells his guests, "I am sometimes ashamed to think that I could not secure myself from vice but by retiring from the exercise of virtue and begin to suspect that I was rather impelled by resentment than led by devotion into solitude."

If wired into the grid, you feel overtaken by resentment if not vice, I hope you can feel and speak your truth without fear of feeling ignorant, being thought crazy, or canceled as a dangerous revolutionary, and unplugging yourself to run off into the woods.

To set the scene for further study and commentary, I would like to begin with a couple of stories, one from the Ivy League, no less.

Creepy Barbies and Ivies

On March 12, 2015, an article appeared in the *Raleigh News and Observer* with the menacing headline, "Creepy Barbie Doll Bad for Kids." It was not a front-page article but ought to have been; it's about "child advocates" protesting against the new "Hello Barbie," which records all the childhood prattle it "hears" during a typical day of play and sends the data "to the Internet cloud" and thus directly to "a toy conglomerate whose only interest in them is financial," observes Susan Linn, executive director of the nonprofit Campaign for a Commercial-Free Childhood.

I am very glad that Ms. Linn voiced her protest, and I wish that she could have been with me in the audience of a conference keynote speech the year before. The prestigious educator, keynote speaker at a prestigious global conference at an Ivy League institution, described a research project his graduate department had planned and directed, in which cameras were to be strapped to children's heads for a day while they went about field trip activities. "They soon forget that the cameras are there," he says, and the cameras record all of their conversation, all day long, and convey it to the researchers. "We learn how they learn," from this conversational plenum (both task-focused and childish prattle), he assures us.

Will we ever see a headline, "Creepy Ivy League Research Bad for Kids"? I doubt it. Where will this research ultimately lead? No doubt, to the adoption of more continuously invasive technology, because everyone knows that if some is good, more must be better. Not content with more limited interviews and assessments, this researcher wants it all—the whole child—and can record her whole brain in order to feed it into the vast data zombie, the techno-industrial-corporate complex taking over education, our last stronghold of intelligent discernment.

There was more to this education researcher's seduction, though. After the creepy camera story, he began to rhapsodize about the smartphone. Soon, he promised, your smartphone will operate "like a miraculous sixth sense" to bring you all kinds of information heretofore unimaginable. But then, in what to me seemed like a contradiction, he added: "Your phone will also be able to filter out all unnecessary data during your day."

In the Q&A that followed, two hands shot up in the audience. The first was a woman of a theological bent who asked him, "Didn't God do well enough when He made our five senses?" I know that you're not supposed to bring the divine into rational argument; however, I thought her question apt enough. I mean, at least logically speaking, wouldn't we have to keep adding new senses to keep expanding our learning if our first five aren't well enough up to the job? Where would be the end of adding senses? How would we carry around all that equipment? I would end up leaving any detachable senses in the coffee shop or lose them under my car seat. Why not use and further develop the senses we already have? That's what we have always called learning.

The second raised hand was my own. "But sir," I began all a-tremble, "I'm a writer. To me, there is no such thing as 'unnecessary data.' I can write a story from a speck on the wall or the way my teakettle whistles. How could I possibly want to be kept from a sensation, or perception, or experience because something else, especially a device, believes it 'unnecessary'?" He paused for a moment before this indignant interrogator. "What is your field?" he asked. "English, language, and literature." "Ah, I see. You deal with fiction while I deal with science." It was clear to me that he meant this not as any kind of put-down but rather as a reasonable explanation of our difference.

What I gathered from him was that, like Robert Oppenheimer with his atom bomb, glutted on scientific conceit and university funding, he felt driven to push on with the quest for better learning mousetraps. The Ivy researcher would see his dream soon realized. Now, every time I turn on my phone or Facebook, I am served an algorithmic chain of what I am supposed to like in ads, articles, information, people—and lord knows what is being kept from me by these feeds. When I have strolled in nature sans device, my archaic five senses have been on high alert to take in data and also, of necessity (due to built-in limitations), filter it out. This has worked well enough for my own purposes, and I do not wish to make the writer's task even more overwhelming by adding new senses to the toolbox. The idea that it would be desirable to carry a phone on such strolls makes me want to blow something up. I can't imagine why anyone who writes would think this a good idea.

As early as 1993, other types of experts were warning us about prescient and controlling technology: "Everything informational and important to the lives of individuals will be found for sale, or for the taking, in cyberspace," foresaw Michael Benedikt in his "Cityspace, Cyberspace, and The Spatiology of Information." Studies now abound about the realization of continuous techno-irruption into our life and consciousness, principally to harvest our data and our money.

The following discussion shares many of these with you, here after I have finally figured out how to air my own shouldn't, I hope in a way that doesn't bring down too much censure if not cancellation. I suppose that if this is now in your hands, I can no longer avoid this censure since a successful piece of writing must of necessity go out on social media, and out there, you can post that puppies and kittens are adorable and bring down a hail of censure. I'm sure that you can by now find me on Instagram, which my students have all assured me I would love. (One especially recommended Reddit for me, and I'm not sure how to take that.) I can guarantee you that even if I loved it, I would still distrust and fear. And this is a distrust and fear not unlike the anti-vaxxers' today. Those anti-teacher conspiracy theorist dinosaurs must also be ignorant, paranoid, or just plain lazy!

What's your point?

My point, at least in part, was, although I didn't realize it at the time, to warn us educators that one day, sooner than we might realize, we would become obsolete. And, as Bill Joy reports in his "Why the Future Doesn't Need Us," "Ray [Kurzweil] said, simply, that the changes would come gradually, and that we would get used to them" (296). Joy's title and Kurzweil's belief both speak compellingly to educators, who have already been demoted from "sage on the stage" to "guide on the side," mere "facilitators" of learning, and might soon slip entirely, along with brick-and-mortar institutions and physical classrooms, into archaism if not nonexistence. (For more coverage of this, see Chapter 3 of my study here, "The Divide Conquers.") This devolution, awareness of which has been supported, so far, by our experience with the COVID-19 pandemic and dependence on online education, might well be fueled by financial reasons: the physical is more expensive than the virtual, at least to the institution, after all. Joy, speaking of technological change in general, contextualizes, "We are aggressively pursuing the promises of these new technologies within the now-unchallenged system of global capitalism and its manifold financial incentives and competitive pressures." While he does not mention education in his essay, again, his point is spot-on for my argument here throughout.

But speaking of archaism, back to the early 'aughts and my initial zeal to come to understand my new master, so I could do its bidding even as my sense and sensibility recoiled. There is a great meme out there showing a pharaoh-like, whip-wielding character standing over a cowering enslaved-person-like character. The latter says, "I don't like this system," and the former responds, "Well, then, why do you stay?" Such is the irony of any protest such as mine today, a concern shared by a great many, as evidenced by all the social media attention to Aldous Huxley's Brave New World prophecy, "People will come to love their oppression, to adore the technologies that undo their capacities to think."

In my conference hopping, I switched from PowerPoint rants to the essay, a cooler approach. In this volume here, you will find the puffed-up title, "A Humanist Educator from the Digital Divide." Humanists, with one sensible shoe permanently grounded in the 19th century, puff themselves up to appear bigger before the oncoming foe. They cling to outmoded notions such as the value of "RL"—real life, with thoughts and feelings connected to biological bodies and public, in-person social experiences.

A more recent compelling source highly recommendable for learning about how our conference keynote speaker's visions of smartphone hijacking have come to pass would be *The Social Dilemma* (2020). This documentary about the level of control social media has over us is so chilling that when I show it to my students, all eventually put down their phones to watch it attentively.

As a child, I loved playing with my Barbie. From childhood to the present, I have loved to walk around the neighborhood and beyond, looking at everything animal, vegetable, and mineral, natural and manmade, and thinking about it all. I have always loved my education and the educating of others. Who will call Surveillance Barbie, smartphones, and education experts creepy? I will, and if you are a bit creeped out right now, read on. With these pages, I do not have your head wired into the Cloud, so I can data-harvest you to hawk more books to you; I just want you to read and think for yourself, in the ancient and reliable way of the humanist.

A Really Good Question(er)

In an argument for a similar power inversion, I read, "If the humanities are to thrive and not just exist in niches of privilege, they will have to visibly demonstrate the contributions to knowledge and society they are making in the digital era." (Digital Humanities). Really—shouldn't "technology" have to prove its value to us?

Today, the humanist instructor finds herself anxiously "wandering between two worlds," backwards and forwards. In Chapter Two, derived from a paper I gave at the same conference where I heard the creepy Ivy keynote, I explore the special situation of the humanist in the digital age via assumptions that underpin education's technology-ecstasy, and I overview ways technology is disrupting our learning and rewiring our theory and practice in ways both demanding and dangerous. Neil Postman has warned that our tendency to ignore both technology's meta-force as cultural change and pop culture's pervasive toxicity can lead to "culture-death." The humanist, especially as educator, has the special charge to meet, with not only healthy skepticism but also constructive practice, this dire and not unreasonable threat. Today, as more technology is pushed as a remedy for pressing education problems, its intersections with economics, creativity, critical thinking, and above all, its force for change in the way we perceive and live, individually and culturally, must be defined and interrogated. Because as a recent author has asserted, "My College Students Are Not OK." Neither are my colleagues, nor much of our society in general. But first, let us hang out with some of my dear friends from the print days of yore. These old humanists had not too much in the way of media beyond the book, no modem or instrument to filter and censor their perceptions and thoughts, and I, for one, am beyond grateful.

CHAPTER 1: A COMPLETE BODY OF ALL ARTS AND SCIENCES"— PRINT CANON PROPHECIES

> For every rational line or forthright statement, there are leagues of senseless cacophony, verbal nonsense, and incoherency.
>
> —Jorge Luis Borges, *The Library of Babel*

If you are an English colleague, you might just have bristled at the word "canon." The canon, or that collection of works assembled by admittedly biased experts and judged as "the best and the brightest," came under attack, when I was in grad school in the 1980s, from the usurper Theory. Arguments such as those emblematized by Deconstruction's challenge not only to texts and words but also to the very alphabet and more practical inquiries such as Stanley Fish's iconoclastic 1982 *Is There a Text in this Class?* demolished the old guard of text-devotees, those who found "a thing of beauty and a joy forever" in the work of the Greats. In the next decade, the Postcolonial movement informed us that much of what we had considered great enough to require in our courses represented the Western colonialist oppressor who had silenced the voices of, if not outright murdered, much of the non-Western world (and certainly any enslaved persons in the Western world). Feminist Theory arose in the smug face of masculinist and sexist literary his-story; a feminist colleague at the university where I taught for a while, looking at my 18th-century syllabus, spat at me, "I wouldn't be caught dead teaching Pope, Swift, and Johnson in my course".

In her own course, she taught obscure women writers of this period. Interesting, yes. Good period coverage, presented without the counterpoint of the patriarchal canon? Hardly. Not only did she need to interrogate and despise their motives—she needed to pariah-tize and strike the canonical greats from your syllabus. This, to me, seemed a great loss to our field and our students. Surely there is room for everyone in our courses, at the least for point-counter-point interpretive energy: keep your friends close, and your enemies closer, as they say.

I was on board, in spirit if not in letter, with most of the intentions and strategies of these movements as their assertions proved unquestionable. In fact, my doctoral special fields are Eighteenth-Century Studies and Feminist Theory. At any rate, it was never my intention in this chapter to discuss grad school boondoggles, so we move on to the point.

OK, we'll get there soon enough. First, I need to mention an enemy to the canon far more formidable, dangerous, and merciless than any critical theorist could ever dream of being—no matter how legitimately offended they might feel about all the insults, impositions, and obstacles canonical history has imposed on their target population (whether textual or human). I refer, of course, to the internet and its comprehensive impact on our intellects and desires.

From my perspective, buttressed by that of the other exceptional scholars who have tackled the challenge, the internet has almost destroyed, or at least seriously challenged, readers' ability to sustain print-literate focus long enough to get through, much less process, the old canonical works. Thus, over the years, I have assigned them less and less. The texts discussed in this chapter at one time starred in their respective courses. But I had to stop including them because no one would or could read them anymore. A new company, Blinkist, now offers "bite-sized bestsellers and book summaries," offering longer works condensed into "15-minute summaries." It has been pointed out that such tools as Cliff Notes have always existed; however, one needed to go out and purchase these at bookstores and drug stores—or visit a brick-and-mortar library to access them. Now, you can, at a keytouch, blink "bite-sized" *War and Peace* onto your screen for a quick classics snack and call it a read. I grind my teeth at the very idea.

Moreover, given the obvious and increasing erosion of my own reader-attention span, I sympathized with my students and opted to choose shorter, easier texts and, in the end, a lot of social media and other purely digital sources. (Instructors early on believed that asking their students to read Milton online would facilitate access to him. Fools! The medium is the message—and on the online medium, the message is that they will just find more distractions, more easily.) What I did was to divide my Brit Lit I students into small groups and have each group cover one book of *Paradise Lost*, incorporating multimedia elements to illustrate and update the continued relevancy of this work; not only did we manage to cover all of PL but also this has remained a superbly successful assignment.

The length, density, vocabulary (complexity and archaisms), and historical contexts of the high-canon works make them, such as they were before Blinkist got hold of them, pretty much unassignable today, tl;dr (for the text-chat uninitiated, "too long; didn't read"), in the populations I have taught. That is, anything outside of the privileged Tier One, and some colleagues there assure me of their own struggles in getting students to read long assignments. This challenge is reported in articles such as "The Elite College Students Who Can't Read Books" (*The Atlantic*, October 1 , 2024). And this is not just an American thing; a colleague guest-teaching at a prestigious European university was told by the department head that a mere "15–20 pages a week of reading, per course, was recommended" for master's degree candidates.

I am not blaming these populations but rather the degradation in our ability to prepare students for college work: the failure of the mentors. At least the literature instructor must find access paths to the classics for her digital natives, and this is a worthy cause for several good reasons. First, these texts themselves are timeless and worthy. Second, because they are timeless, our students can and will connect with them if guided patiently. This chapter features not only my own musings but also, and especially, those of my students from various courses where we undertook these texts. These courses include British and World Literatures as well as my Composition 2 (analysis of literary works) special topics 'Dystopia' course.

Although I cannot now, due to time's erosion of both records and memories, give specific credit to individual students for some ideas included here, I want to acknowledge my students' role in these discussions. Our inquiry here, what some of the greats over the past eight hundred years would have thought about the internet, ever proved an enthusiastic one for my students and gave them sharp insights into how these authors predicted, described, and warned us about our new digital masters. I hope you enjoy these now as much as we did, in my classes of ever-curious pupils who just needed a way out of the dark forest of doubt and resistance and into the light of these authors' genius. My course evaluations frequently featured the praise, "She can bring old works up into the light of the present and help us learn what they can still teach us today." I did that? My work here has meant something.

What follows features these authors, their words, and our interpretations of them vis-à-vis our own interrogations of the digital paradigm shift. From these highest-canon greats, we can glean the following:

- John Milton, *Paradise Lost*, or how Satan came up with the greatest weapon possible against God and his favorite creation, us;
- Jonathan Swift, *Gulliver's Travels*, or how the internet actually works, simply stated;
- Jorge Luis Borges, "The Library of Babel," or why the internet more accurately describes our universe than the print canon has done or can do;
- Stanislaw Lem, "Non Serviam," or the false freedom and easy end of the Metaverse; and saving the best for last,
- Dante Alighieri, *Inferno*, or how the smartphone will deliver you, unrepentant, to all nine circles of hell.

Many other canonical works can be fruitfully harvested for predictions of and allusions to our dubious reality today. These are a few of our favorites, and I hope you enjoy our interpretations. If you have your own to contribute, I will gladly receive them, as finding reasons everywhere, diachronically and synchronically, and especially among genius, to fear and distrust the internet is a chief hobby nowadays.

From a casual perspective, we start with Milton's Satan, who planned the war. Next, Swift invented its "engine." Borges provides the geography, and Lem the economics. Finally, from Dante, the theology: we imagine divine punishment of our cyber sins. Our discussion features the scholarly and the secular, with a lot of creative license and a dash of comedy. We hope you learn just how timeless the classics can be. And again, many thanks to students over the years in British and World Literatures, not to mention Dystopian Lit, for their insights and efforts reflected here.

John Milton, Paradise Lost, Book 2

Seventeenth-century superstar John Milton creates the second-greatest (next to Dante's *Inferno*) literary hell, populated by chief rebel angel Lucifer—now Satan—and the other fallen ones who dared challenge God in a war on heaven. These, having in Book One awakened from their punitive fall to the bottom of creation—that point furthest from God—chained in a vast lake of fire, naturally want to find a way out. So, in Book Two, they convene to try to find this way. "Satan debates whether another Battel be to be hazarded for the recovery of Heaven: some advise it, others dissuade" (Book 2 Argument).

The dissuaders reject, for example, renewed war, too dangerous, and conciliatory efforts, too useless. Finally, Satan himself comes up with a foolproof plan:

> What if we find
> Some easier enterprize? There is a place [345]
> (If ancient and prophetic fame in Heav'n
> Err not) another World, the happy seat
> Of some new Race call'd Man, about this time
> To be created like to us, though less
> In power and excellence, but favour'd more   [350]
> Of him who rules above; so was his will
> Pronounc'd among the Gods, and by an Oath,
> That shook Heav'ns whol circumference, confirm'd.
> Thither let us bend all our thoughts, to learn
> What creatures there inhabit, of what mould,   [355]
> Or substance, how endu'd, and what thir Power,
> And where thir weakness, how attempted best,
> By force or suttlety: Though Heav'n be shut,
> And Heav'ns high Arbitrator sit secure
> In his own strength, this place may lye expos'd
> The utmost border of his Kingdom, left
> To their defence who hold it: here perhaps
> Som advantagious act may be achiev'd
> By sudden onset, either with Hell fire
> To waste his whole Creation, or possess   [365]
> All as our own, and drive as we were driven,
> The punie habitants, or if not drive,
> Seduce them to our Party, that thir God
> May prove thir foe, and with repenting hand
> Abolish his own works...

When I asked my class, "What do you imagine would be the best weapon Satan could use against mankind, to bring about our fall from grace?" The first response was "Walmart," surely a contender. But this was immediately followed by "the internet." They homed in on "what thir power and what thir weakness, how attempted best by force or suttlety." Students pointed out that humans' "power" could lead them to ceaseless and successful efforts for a stronger internet, while their "weakness" would cause them to use this ever-growing power for useless, stupid, and violent ends. As for the choice between "force or suttlety," a clear answer joined Milton's/Satan's hand to that of Aldous Huxley and then Neil Postman in other, much later coups of prophecy:

> There will be, in the next generation or so, a pharmacological method of making people love their servitude, and producing dictatorship without tears, so to speak, producing a kind of painless concentration camp for entire societies, so that people will in fact have their liberties taken away from them, but will rather enjoy it, because they will be distracted from any desire to rebel by propaganda or brainwashing, or brainwashing enhanced by pharmacological methods. And this seems to be the final revolution. (Aldous Huxley, Tavistock Group, California Medical School, 1961)

The mass doping of our modern society through pharmaceuticals: antidepressants, opioids, Adderal, and the like (praise to all for the unquestionable help they do give to the suffering) has indeed occurred and needs no elaboration here. However, it is inefficient as not all people choose to take drugs, and there is an unnecessarily cumbersome and often expensive process of getting people onto these psychotropics or, failing legal prescription, the risks incumbent on street crime. That is, compared to the relatively great ease of getting them all online and clutching phones to their faces 24/7.

What Orwell feared were those who would ban books. What Huxley feared was that there would be no reason to ban a book, for there would be no one who wanted to read one. Orwell feared those who would deprive us of information. Huxley feared those who would give us so much that we would be reduced to passivity and egoism. Orwell feared that the truth would be concealed from us. Huxley feared the truth would be drowned in a sea of irrelevance. Orwell feared we would become a captive culture. Huxley feared we would become a trivial culture . . . As Huxley remarked in Brave New World Revisited, the civil libertarians and rationalists who are ever on the alert to oppose tyranny 'failed to take into account man's almost infinite appetite for distractions' . . . In short, Orwell feared that what we hate will ruin us. Huxley feared that what we love will ruin us. (Postman, *Amusing Ourselves to Death*)

If you believe Postman, and what observant person wouldn't, it's an easy hop to realizing that the internet is the ultimate drug, one almost all of us willingly, gladly, continuously consume. Satan well understood, from personal experience, that "tyrants are apt to produce rebels" (David Hume, "Of Love and Marriage"). So his weapon cannot be off-putting. I would ask my class, "If you saw some big monster, fiery red and maggoty, run at you with pitchforks, chains and hellfire, what would you do?" The universal answer must be, "RUN!!" "Now, how many of you have a smartphone?" Milton's Satan devised his best comeback to his foe and rival God and the newly-minted mankind, an "advantageous act . . . to waste his whole creation . . .

[and] seduce them to our party." Bill Joy has observed, "I think it is no exaggeration to say we are on the cusp of the further perfection of extreme evil, an evil whose possibility spreads well beyond that which weapons of mass destruction bequeathed to the nation-states, on to a surprising and terrible empowerment of extreme individuals" (Skrbina, *Confronting Technology*, 298). And how else, or at least better, for this to happen than through that "act" that has divided and conquered us all? For example on social media, Satan's act has empowered every individual, extremist to just plain ignorant, to advertise their own opinion, waging as Thomas Hobbes observed centuries ago, the "war of every man against every man." This act has allowed a global cyber-breeding-ground for terrorist training and transaction. In his revenge, Satan ensured for us a mortal sin of which we remain unrepentant, aside from a lot of lip service. The best contemporary prophets assure us that the techno-vehicle of this sin is going nowhere but forward, ever-increasing in power. In spite of its failure in theological terms, Milton's Pandemonium celebrates its practical success.

To learn specifically how the internet can and likely will specifically seduce and waste God's favorite, casting into doubt His divine wisdom, make sure to catch the Dante discussion a bit later. But first, let us meet "the engine" of doom.

To learn specifically how the internet can and likely will seduce and waste God's favorite—us, casting into doubt His divine wisdom, after all— make sure to catch the Dante discussion a bit later. But first, let us meet "the engine."

Jonathan Swift, Gulliver's Travels *Book 3*

It seems that the first actual "computer" came to us in a literary icon of satire, Swift's *Gulliver's Travels*. On his visit to the Academy of Lagado (his requisite swipe at education and science), Gulliver encounters a professor and his students obsessed with the "engine" depicted in Swift's drawing (via Wikipedia).

> Students were charged with turning ceaselessly the cross-poles, on which were attached cards with words on them; as these words continuously fell randomly from the poles, scribes scribbled down the "sentences" created. Using these, the professor himself would ultimately transact the world's most significant project:

> Six hours a day the young students were employed in this labour; and the professor showed me several volumes in large folio, already collected, of broken sentences, which he intended to piece together,

and out of those rich materials, to give the world a complete body of all arts and sciences; which, however, might be still improved, and much expedited, if the public would raise a fund for making and employing five hundred such frames in Lagado, and oblige the managers to contribute in common their several collections.

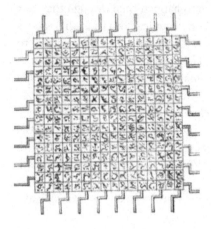

The scholarly community has shown a mild interest in Swift's "computing engine," offered in Gulliver's Travels Book 3, his direct assault on the follies of higher learning and especially science. Scientists have especially noted the engine's place in computation history, and literary scholars have explored the puzzle of exactly who and what, specifically, Swift was satirizing with it.

My interest being more general, I point first to the fund-raising requirement. Anyone who has spent time at a university knows of grant culture, where the most desirable department members are those who bring in money because it takes a lot of money to do science, a quasi-irony addressed by Stanislaw Lem in his "Non Serviam."

My students and I were more interested in the engine's function to generate endless strings of "broken sentences . . . to give the world a complete body of all arts and sciences." One blurted out, "Hey—isn't that what the internet is doing?" And it did seem so; its monocular proponents have viewed it as education's magic wand, putting all knowledge at every student's fingertips. In later chapters, we will consider a few specific cases of such magic thinking: MIT's One Laptop Per Child project, and "hack-schooling," a phenomenon launched by privileged and obviously talented Logan LaPlante, who at thirteen gave us a TED Talk that "disrupted" the whole idea and project of education, to that point. With only his laptop and a Starbucks, tween Logan could learn enough to change the world and topple my own.

Because after all, why listen to centuries of well-educated and experienced experts in their field when you can get the Way from a thirteen-year-old? The former takes much time and effort, the latter takes the average TED Talker ten minutes.

We will discuss hackschooling at length a bit later, but for now I can conclude this section with Swift's Gulliver, who gave us here possibly the best description of the internet's apparent true promise, what anyone with a laptop in a Starbucks can accomplish: "Every one knew how laborious the usual method is of attaining to arts and science; whereas, by his contrivance, the most ignorant person, at a reasonable charge, and with a little bodily labour, might write books in philosophy, poetry, politics, laws, mathematics, and theology, without the least assistance from genius or study." (I can feel Swift spinning in his grave as he considers AI and ChatGPT.) I myself wrote my doctoral dissertation on a typewriter while digging up musty tomes from dank libraries; however, for this effort currently underway, I have used the internet as a primary tool. I cannot overstress how helpful it is for delivering knowledge to one's fingertips. Whether that knowledge is effectively transmitted to, and processed by my brain, I will leave to my readers. I do like to believe that I have approached its use if not with the benefit of genius, at least with that of study. A quick glance at the state of information out there today, though, informs us that neither is too much required any longer. If I could bring any one writer back for a day, it would have to be Swift, although I might not survive the 24 hours of riotous laughing—mixed with some heady Swiftian satire—as I showed him around our current idiocrasy.

Jorge Luis Borges, The Library of Babel

Not being able to help it, as per my regrettable habit, upon first awakening today I reached for my phone and learned that Kanye West claims never to have read a book. Thinking how grim my own life would have been had I not read a million books, I was pleased to see the Comments highly critical of West's lapse. (I surf Facebook not for its primary content, I tell myself, but for the Comments. I do this as a critical-thinking exercise, I tell myself.) Apparently, things aren't entirely hopeless out there, not yet at least. Of course, the Kanye story could just be Fake News...

Venturing from my bed to my den, I flipped on the TV and the news. I learned that "book-banning is at an all-time high." Any books having to do with "race, gender or sexuality" are targeted for removal from school libraries. I am thinking that this would entail removing at least half of all books, and as has been astutely pointed out, principally the Bible. Certainly we must strike all Greco-Roman mythologies and their influences, as Zeus/Jupiter was nothing if not a predatory rapist whose appearance anywhere should be triggering.

As a kid, I lived for my mom's begrudging weekly drive to the public library, where I checked out books on a range of subjects mostly scientific: dinosaurs, astronomy, geology, botany, and studies of the animal population (my favorite having been the aardvark, for which I developed a ten-year-old's passion that is with me still). We could check out a maximum of six books, which I would finish in three days and start begging mom for a return trip. As she begrudged even the weekly necessity, you know how this was received.

Later in my teens, I graduated to the great writers. Among these, I loved Borges from the first sentence: "I owe the discovery of Uqbar to the conjunction of a mirror and an encyclopedia." The top of my head nearly blew off. A couple of sentences later: "...mirrors and copulation are abominable because they increase the number of men," I nearly fainted with delight ("Tlon, Uqbar, Orbis Tertius"). I got hooked from here on Borges, the ultimate philosopher of fake news; his writings are full of lying scholars, illusory images, contradictory facts, and so on. "The Library of Babel" became a favorite although it overwhelmed me with its yank out from under me of the rug of any certainty of any kind. (Luckily, I got to grad school about the time Deconstruction and Postmodernism seized power, so I got to build a solid theoretical foundation for our current scene of fakery and disinformation.)

Jonathan Haidt, in his 2022 *Atlantic* article "Why the Past 10 Years of American Life Have Been Uniquely Stupid," compares this brand of stupid to the story of the Tower of Babel, where God punished mankind's pride and ingratitude by condemning humans to speak many different languages and thus prove incoherent with each other. Frightful discord followed, and still does, the price of fragmentation and isolation. Haidt's substack has the title of *Life After Babel: Adapting to a World We Can No Longer Share*, which boils the threat down nicely. Satan's plan has worked well: isolate them, make them unable to communicate constructively with each other, goad and train them to kill each other—a hell on earth if there ever could be one. "Now is the time of monsters," proclaimed Antonio Gramsci, in another context addressing that "interregnum" or period of time between two rulers.

But Satan could not accomplish his work without something to build on, and that something must be seductive. How do you ruin a library, that most benign and loveable of institutions, and turn it against its devotees and against the aims of knowledge, understanding and peace? Book banning is one way; but to-date, wherever it has been attempted, it has had too many opponents. The easier answer is just make it infinite. "When it was announced that the Library contained all books, the first reaction was unbounded joy. All men felt themselves the possessors of an intact and secret treasure. There was no personal problem, no world problem, whose eloquent solution did not exist . . . The universe was justified; the universe suddenly became congruent with the unlimited width and breadth of humankind's hope" (Borges).

When people had only physical, brick-and-mortar libraries, their research potential, however great (depending on the size and budget of the institution), proved limited. However much grandeur and pride the scholar might have felt, this met necessary limitations imposed by the physical universe. I recall my overwhelming gratitude at the interlibrary loan opportunity: if you were willing to wait days, or weeks, you could acquire some tomes outside of your zip code. The scholar, semi-sated by their efforts, survived on dual hope and fear: another book would appear on their subject, to feed their research stockpile; and, another book would appear on their subject, to eclipse their own or put them at risk of redundancy or worse yet, plagiarism, however inadvertent.

The Library of Babel, being infinite, allowed even the greatest of scholars to slip down the hellish channels of contention, the sluices of self-interest, the self-contradictions of infinite potential. "Thousands of greedy individuals abandoned their sweet native hexagons and rushed downstairs, upstairs, spurred by their vain desire to find their Vindication. These pilgrims squabbled in the narrow corridors, muttered dark imprecations, strangled one another on the divine staircases, threw deceiving volumes down ventilator shafts, were themselves hurled to their deaths by men of distant regions. Others went insane..." (Borges).

My fledgling philosophical consciousness, at the age of eighteen when I first devoured Borges, followed all of his labyrinths and contradictions and especially that of the Library, which proved both "the formless and chaotic nature of virtually all books" and the fact that "it includes not a single absolute piece of nonsense." Its infinite nature preempts the possibility of untruth and the problem of Fake News, because "There is no combination of characters one can make—*dhcmrlchtdj*, for example—that the divine Library has not foreseen and that in one or more of its secret tongues does not hide a terrible significance." Truth must yield sway to significance. How better describe the internet?

"Methodical composition distracts me from the present condition of humanity," writes the Library's narrator. If we can understand Haidt's Babel as the breakdown of truths into significances (and how can we argue, without risk of prejudice, invidiousness and censorship, that anyone's idea is not significant?) then we can easily see how the internet's promise of infinite knowledge can be weaponized. If all "hackschooler" Logan LaPlante needs is his laptop and a seat at Starbucks to produce a disruption to the whole history of education, where does that leave those of us who prefer our education a bit more organized, if not supervised, by the already knowledge-able? Heresy, you shout! Get rid of teachers and schools; multiply laptops and Starbucks! After all, kids must buy their own devices, and someone else pays the coffeehouse bills. In fact, who needs the public space? Each to their own Hexagon, as my favorite non-traceable (seriously, and if it doesn't show up on Google—does it exist? Did I dream it?) quotation goes: "plugged into his or her own video display terminal, frantically sending and receiving messages that have no meaning because there is no more context."

Context and thus temporal, spatial, physical and psychic limits have no logical place in the infinite Library. "The Library is a sphere whose exact center is any hexagon and whose circumference is unattainable." I think of Mark Bauerlein's simple but strong assertion that while it is indeed pretty to think that students spend their vast connected time seeking useful knowl-edge, they just don't. Why would they, when they have each other's lives and likes to explore? When they have nothing short of Everything, Everywhere to explore? I cannot say that even, or especially, as an egghead teenager given the internet portal, I wouldn't have been glued to it. In fact, I feel certain I would have been; it would have saved my mom that vexing biweekly trip to the brick and mortar library downtown.

I am reminded of the 1997 sci-fi-horror film *Event Horizon*. The eponymous spaceship has, through transgressive pride coupled with the unrestrained quest for knowledge, managed to equip itself with technology powerful enough to pop itself into "hell." This hell is chiefly characterized by entirely random extreme violence, sadism and torture, all irrationally inflicted by the crew members on each other along with visions of the same from each member's personal circle. I consulted with my students, some of whom had seen and loved the film. (We could not watch it together, however, due to its overly disturbing imagery and content; I myself remain semi-traumatized by it twenty-five years later.) What exactly was the scariest thing about it? My class deduced that this "hell," achieved by man's scientific reach beyond his grasp, was none other than chaos, that formless and infinite realm outside the universe conceived by its very name as "the many (safely) organized and contained in the one." The black-hole-powered ship had popped itself through the universe's membrane and into chaos, where there is no order, truth, meaning, or empathy, which depends at least half on logic. In Babel, in the Faustian bargain, the perpetrators directly defy God's rational limits on man's power and end up in hell. We do this indirectly with technology. But, I reminded my students, don't we scorn if not despise rules, order, commands; homework, grades, professors? Don't we hate those who make us put away our cellphones during class? Don't we curse the very oppressions imposed where we sit now, in this classroom and institution? Yeah, they hesitantly affirmed, but the alternative, none of this, is far worse. They might feel oppressed, victimized by the system, but they definitely are not unaware of the consequences of losing it.

What happened in the Library? "Epidemics, heretical discords, pilgrimages that inevitably degenerate into brigandage have decimated the population. I believe I mentioned the suicides, which are more and more frequent every year." Read the news, folks. Truth, logic, order, limits might not rationally exist in the infinite Library. But we want infinite possibility; who needs these old constraints? The Library is what it is, and we will find the technologies to blast through its illusory dimensions, if it kills us, destroying every peacekeeping if provisional truth, along with way. "I suspect that the human species . . . teeters at the verge of extinction, yet that the Library—enlightened, solitary, infinite, perfectly unmoving, armed with precious volumes, pointless, incorruptible, and secret—will endure." And technology proceeds apace, concludes David Skrbina in his *The Metaphysics of Technology*, irresistibly seductive and unstoppable in its portal to the Everything, Everywhere.

Stanislaw Lem, "Non Serviam"

"[T]he cruelest science man ever created." Lem's narrator refers to personetics, the creation in labs of artificial beings and worlds. Could we say the same about Artificial Intelligence? (We remember poor HAL in *2001: A Space Odyssey*. What could go wrong?) Lem wrote "Non Serviam" in 1971 when such a science existed mostly in fantasy and sci-fi. Now, it seems that we have arrived. Consider the recent hysteria about AI ChatGPT, which apparently has in its infinite ability the capability to "destroy college" or at least the college assignment, essay and otherwise.

Lem's tale tracks the rise and fall of a group of scientists who succeed in programming and launching a new creation: like Eden, only mathematical in nature. Essentially, it's the apotheosis of all computer programs. As this world stems and branches, and grows and develops, thinks and philosophizes and feels, its laboratory creators, its "god," watches from above, presumably sitting with coffee and a sandwich at the computer screen. The personoids, of course, are about as empirically aware of their creator as we are of ours. Herein lies the fun that Lem likely intended in the story. However, living in the digital takeover of my own world now, I have focused on the weakest link in this megalomaniacal scheme of science. Read on.

Mark Zuckerberg popped "Metaverse" onto the scene. In this magic realm, humans transform into cyber-explorers, transcending the physical boundaries of our limited and dull world. Of course, doing so can be awkward and expensive, but who cares if it's the new frontier?

A quick scroll down Meta's Facebook page shows stories of overcoming all kinds of limits and finding all joys in our new metaverse. My attention, however, settled on the top right screen corner: a blue box with "View Shop" in it. Back within a familiar boundary: you have to buy all this. Wikipedia states the case baldly, up-front: "According to Meta, the 'metaverse' refers to the integrated environment that links all of the company's products and services." The rest of the Wikipedia article is devoted to Meta as the extreme business venture it is.

So what is the Metaverse? My Google search revealed mostly business talk. I came across a few commentaries on its predictable dangers: over-immersion, addiction, escapism, and the physical inconveniences of never moving your body or shopping for, cooking and eating healthy food—a virtual body needs no nourishment aside from the "mathematical" sort upon which Lem's personoids rely. But my favorite I found again in Wikipedia, about how the wiser among us "would be more positive towards metaverse development if it was not dominated by 'companies and disaster capitalists trying to figure out a way to make more money as the real world's resources are dwindling.'" As always, *cui bono*. Rather than trying to fix and help our current real world, why not blast us all, at a hefty fee of course, into virtual worlds? This logic reminds me of our current education predicament: rather than invest in the public education mandated by no less than Thomas Jefferson, why not start a bunch of new profit-driven private schools, online diploma mills and homeschools at Starbucks? There are now all kinds of classrooms out there, where all kinds of weirdness and failures occur because there is no control. I know, I know...shouldn't we have the freedom to choose? It's complicated.

In their imaginations and from their desires, humans can create all kinds of worlds to explore, be thrilled, find superior ways of being and living. We have traditionally called this "art." In art, we can enjoy the best of both worlds: our necessary physical one and our boundless imaginative one. In fact, this balance seems ideal. So why weaken or even destroy one for the sake of the other? This might actually be the main thesis and research question of my entire book here. Since I am irrevocably bound to my physical body (and, at my age, this weighs more heavily, literally and figuratively, than ever before), if I had to choose, I'd destroy the virtual world. After all we'd still have paper, canvas, musical instruments, stages, film and much more. These have sustained and delighted us for millennia. Yes, bring on the new cyber-stuff; however, this new cyberworld hauls with it an unavoidable invidiousness grounded in its incredible powers of seduction and potential for addiction. The fleshly realm is awkward, painful, shameful, and ever deteriorating. Wouldn't it be so much better to be cyber? Lem's personoids seem to enjoy both ontologies as they are simultaneously experiencing fully developed "lives" while "living" off the pure infallibility of their mathematical programming. So what's the big deal?

The big deal is that there really is no change, and the promise is illusory beyond some perceptual frissons. A metaphysical God did not create the metaverse; a highly motivated human capitalist did. Lem tells us right away that everything that happens in the new creation is "subject to discretionary control on the part of the experimenter." The world itself is "built of mathematics," O.K, could be interesting—"though the building blocks of that mathematics are ordinary, perfectly physical objects—relays, transistors, logic circuits—in a word, the whole huge network of the digital machine." I myself am still trying to understand how mining cryptocurrency can produce so much real pollution. Isn't that disappointing, that your enchanted avatar is still just bumping around in a perfectly human thing? And this super-personoid avatar need not pump itself up too much about its own capabilities; as Lem explains, "It would behave in a manner perfectly logical, always consistent, lucid, and well ordered, and it might even seem, to a human observer, a genius in creative action and decision making. But it could in no way be a man, for it would be bereft of his mysterious depth, his internal intricacies, his labyrinthine nature..." He might as well be describing the "writing" of ChatGPT.

We 21st-century humans like to imagine that we can do better. Zuckerberg would hardly count on profits from an inefficient product. As AI proponents today speculate about machines that are learning more and more to think like us, can they ever? Logically no, because their creators would have to make them flawed, deceitful, easy to seduce, capable of terrible decisions, frightful cruelties and horrific mistakes. Plus, such a machine would want to dominate, oppress, torture and slaughter us as we have done each other ceaselessly, throughout history. Do we want a machine that can think "like us"? God, no, something better, please. Then what? Lem joins Swift and Borges in his final judgment of such a man-made thinking machine, that in its thoughts and pronouncements will "still be closer to a billion chattering parrots—howsoever brilliantly trained the parrots be—than to the simplest, most stupid man." Do we have any way out of our simplicity and stupidity? Do we want a way? Maybe through deliberate acts of kindness and charity; maybe through yoga and meditation; maybe through an organic diet; maybe even through religion or at least some kind of faith in a better, kinder, more charitable world. I myself will never look for anything better in a machine unless, perhaps I think about my coffee maker. Now that is one fancy and skilled machine, but there are better Italian models out there.

We are still not at the best reason to doubt the promise of Lem's personoid creation and Zuck's metaverse. That reason we have glanced and hinted at, but let us allow Lem to explain it, as he ends his tale: "The bills for the electricity consumed have to be paid quarterly, and the moment is going to come when my university superiors demand the 'wrapping up' of the experiment—that is, the disconnecting of the machine, or, in other words, the end of the world." Yes, the world ends not with a bang or a whimper—but with withdrawn funding and a pulled plug.

Ian Bogost entitles his *Atlantic* article: "The Metaverse Is Bad: It is Not a World in a Headset but a Fantasy of Power" (October 21, 2021). I had read about a third of another *Atlantic* article, whose title unfortunately now escapes me (even on Google) before I realized that it was satirical. Or was it? It described a culture in which the haves could afford the equipment needed for VL existence while the have-nots, left behind, had to make do in the real-life squalor and deprivation. In other words, just like normal in capitalist society. *Cui bono?* Remember that this is one primary definition of digital divide: as usual, the unequal competition for survival between the haves and have-nots. We might be superior to "chattering parrots"; however, I don't trust us enough yet, if ever, to do anything that does not foundationally involve power and money. In later chapters, I shall direct this informed cynicism to the realm of education. With the takeover of machines designed by the surveilling gods, I am afraid that education has not progressed much beyond Swift's Academy of Lagado. And Lem's title, translated "I will not serve," has taken on new context, strength and threat in the digital economy.

Dante's Inferno

I did promise Dante, but I am not worthy. At least, I'm not up to it. He is my master, who, if I let him, leads me out of my own dark forest and through my hell, teaching me a customized Purgatory and giving me hope in the fact that I can save myself by repenting my sins and working my way out of them, ever looking to the light, which is profoundly NOT electronic.

Perhaps this whole volume is about working through Purgatory, though I doubt the outcome can be Paradise. Maybe just a place without screens? We have loved them, but that love is returned in the form of venal seduction, if not our pathways to ruin.

So here, I've decided to turn the commentary over to my students. We read the *Inferno* in World Lit I, and since Dante can be daunting—even for those of us in the biz—I decided to assign them a task: show how the internet can seduce us into all nine levels of hell. The results were even richer and wittier than I can transmit here via my paraphrases; however, all credit to my World Lit I class for these insights. So here goes:

- First Circle (Limbo)—occupied by the "virtuous pagans" and the unbaptized who unfortunately came into the world before Christ, a raw deal if ever there was one. Who occupies this one? "My parents, who have no idea how to use a smartphone—theirs has big numbers, and they call each other on it—or the internet, which my mom uses for recipes. They possess but are guiltless in use."
- Second Circle (Lust)—occupied by those overcome by lust. "This one's easy. Getting caught texting your side chick is hell enough!" I don't doubt it.
- Third Circle (Gluttony)—"Does spending too much time scrolling your phone and playing video games count?" "How much do you spend?" "Oh, 6–8 hours per day." Yes, that counts.
- Fourth Circle (Greed)—"I'd say it's having to get a new upgrade every year just because they put one out. That, and have you seen those mountains of thrown-away electronics? They say poor kids crawl all over those, forced to retrieve some of the valuable materials in there, and they die of terrible diseases from that. I'd say that's about greed, all right." I couldn't agree more.
- Fifth Circle (Anger)—"I mean, just check out the Comments section. You could write that you love sitting in flowers and petting kittens, and someone will viciously attack you for crushing the flowers and not choosing dogs." Point made and well-illustrated.
- Sixth Circle (Heresy)—"Wouldn't the 'heretics' in this case, nowadays, be people like you, Professor, who hate the internet?" Yes, and oops....
- Seventh Circle (Violence)—"It seems like so much of the messed-up violence in the world has roots in the internet. People get 'radicalized,' people post violent videos that inspire others to do the same, there's all sorts of emotional violence done there. And isn't cyber bullying, aren't the suicides in this circle? It's said that social media have caused a big uptick in

teen suicides. So yeah, this one's pretty obvious." And this one's done her homework, for sure.

- Eighth Circle (Fraud)—"You've got to be so careful online; every day I get all these bogus emails and texts trying to get me to buy some bullshit or other. And those who hack your identity or your bank information online. And then there's phishing, catfishing, black fishing. Oh, and Instagram filters that make someone look like a whole 'nuther, and prettier, person. There's pretty much no end to the fraud you can commit, and easily, online." The internet's potential for fraud might just be its most hellish aspect.
- Ninth Circle (Treachery)—"Well, according to you, Professor Sapp, we've even sold your 'religion,' education, to the post-capitalist cyber surveillance state, for the sake of profit and the plunder of young wallets, minds and souls." A+ to you, sir—and mercy for us all.

For the past millennium, the greats have been warning us. Fortunately for our false peace of mind today, so many are unaware of these warnings because they are "too long, didn't read." If only these prophets could return today, for even one hour, to post their warnings on Insta—though from what I understand, Reddit might accommodate them better. The *Inferno* dramatized on TikTok? Why not? I'm sure someone out there can stop filming their pets, cooking or efforts to concoct a new rainbow toilet-cleaner long enough to give it a try. It could beat Blinkist in followers, I'm sure.

CHAPTER 2: WANDERING BETWEEN TWO WORLDS: A "HUMANIST" LAMENTATION

> Wandering between two worlds, one dead,
> The other powerless to be born,
> With nowhere yet to rest my head,
> Like these, on earth I wait forlorn.
> Their faith, my tears, the world deride—
> I come to shed them at their side.
>
> —Matthew Arnold, "Stanzas from the Grande Chartreuse"

My book and this chapter title reflect my experience and feeling as both a "print native" and an English instructor today, with one big difference: Arnold called his worlds "one dead and the other powerless to be born," whereas the humanist instructor's print world is far from dead—in fact, the bulk of our district syllabi for all courses still heavily calls for print literacy—and the digital world is a demanding, wildly experimental child already.

Not only wandering between but also compromising these two worlds is daunting and wearying along with challenging and exciting; any humanist should agree that if it's a human enterprise, it falls within our scope and duty. As a humanist, I accept the charge and even the claim that digital rhetoricians assert, that "...all writing [today] is computer mediated; all writing is digital," or at least potentially and perhaps even ideally so in our current zeitgeist. "Writing today means weaving text, images, sound and video—working within and across multiple media, often for delivery within and across digital spaces." This reads like the frequent professional-development sessions I must attend in which I am urged to "address all the learning styles," "go where my students already are," and "keep them engaged." What better way than taking them to the digital arcade? "And, perhaps now more so than ever before, writing requires a deep attention to context, audience, and meaning making across the multiple tools and media available to us as writers" (DigiRhet.org). These are all familiar terms to English instructors, and the implied hermeneutical cyber-circling is supposed to be well within our powers.

English instructors tend to believe that most problems are essentially semantic. We must figure out just how far "humanism" can stretch before it no longer has much to do with being "human." One of the early techno-apocalyptics, Mark Slouka, issues dire warnings about the cyber-dehuman-ization of mankind: "Like shined deer, we seem to be wandering en masse onto the digital highway, and the only concern heard in the land, by and large, is that some of us may be left behind" (9), pointing to our wholesale buying-in to what he eventually calls "the hive": one single cyber-mind with no tolerance for individuality, creativity or critical thinking—the classic humanist desiderata. Slouka echoes his obvious master, Neil Postman (1986), who threatens, "To be unaware that a technology comes equipped with a program for social change, to maintain that technology is neutral, to make the assumption that technology is always a friend to culture is, at this late hour, stupidity plain and simple" and apocalyptically prophesies that in a nation addicted to a continuous and undistinguishable mainline of online trivia, disguised as information, "culture-death is a real possibility" (*Amusing Ourselves* 68). A quick look at our current political climate, especially in this election year, reveals the reification of Postman's prophecy.

Social change, friend to culture, and the unveiled call to preserve what-ever the "social" and "culture" are (presumably print-literate-logic, judging by the rest of Postman's argument) are surely the humanist's vocabulary and arena. In fact, a host of techno-apocalyptic humanists from Postman to Nich-olas Carr seem to draw energy, if not purpose, from a traditional dualist us-v.-them mentality, with the humanist responsible for saving mankind from the cyber-borg even though, as we all know here, resistance is futile. However, books are sold and careers sustained as humanist resistance fighters, at least so far; and this critical battle front can reinforce a techno-besieged humani-ties platform with sufficient raison d'être to guarantee survival for a while, one imagines if not hopes. Hence this volume you now hold and peruse.

But a more compelling definition challenge is that of "technology" itself: what can the humanist make of such as "technology," "digital natives," the "digital divide"? Definition must always be the first task. Let's start by looking at the phrase "digital native." I myself am not supposed to be one, having only ramped onto the i-way in the last two decades of my six-decade existence whereas my students, for the most part, had a device of some sort stuck in their hands as soon as they could consciously make a fist. And this putative distinction creates the definition of "digital divide," which usually means access to computer technology, whereas I want now to use the definition of conscious buy-in to the digital world. My students are supposed to be consciously, purposively digital-age disciples, and thus desiring and expecting all their learning to be offered on it; their instructor, on the other hand, is a dinosaur whose "sage-on-the-stage" teaching method of assigning textbook chapters and providing notes about these from a podium betrays her obvious mental desiccation and need to go, to paraphrase Joyce's Molly Bloom, out on the paper-and-podium ash-heap.

Neil Postman saw little if any difference between television and the internet, albeit he did see it in its earlier avatars: aside from speed and saturation, the same phenomenon of video simulacrum of reality, in that its images are reproducible and dependent on perceiver manipulation but more continuously available, interactive and stimulating. Having grown up with television and thus addiction to the video simulacrum, I am a lot more at home in cyberspace than the dividers might want to admit. As for my digital-native students, they pretty much refuse to do their assignments any more readily on their devices than they would on paper. Neil Postman believed that the video simulacrum, in his case television, should be uniquely for entertainment; so following his logic, that is what young folks should use the internet screens for: following each other's antics on social media. However, students have recently informed me that they do most of their learning on YouTube and now TikTok. (When I asked students asked why they preferred TikTok over YouTube, one opined, "YouTube is so slow, and you have to listen to too much story.")

Along with these other digital-divide definitions, we need to acknowledge a medium-divide challenge: the instructor's requirement to study, learn and choose appropriate learning media for her students' best access and performance. And this has proven tricky, if not often tragic: too many prolonged battles between the instructor trying to get students off their devices long enough to do classwork, not to mention homework once we send them back out into the world. Then, there are those who advocate putting them on video games and TikTok (and now, alas, AI) as formal learning platforms, touting the superior successes of working with students where they most like to be or are at least thought most likely to be, playing games and cyber surfing. I have seen this medium-divide issue as both a source of frustration and a professional development opportunity; moreover, no one, not even the new digital gods, argues that print literacy is "dead," and its ways cannot be ignored any more than the new digital ways can be.

In education at least, I'm a lover, not a fighter. I have never tried to make my students put away their phones. After a couple of years of feeling help-less before the new mesmeric distraction device they all brought into my classroom, I started to give my students the choice of whether to use their smartphones in class or keep them put away during our predominantly lecture-discussion classes. And guess what? A good majority voted for the latter, the rest benignly conceded, and almost all reported a better class experience overall, resting from their cyber-marathon for at least that hour. Although technology educator-gurus from Clay Shirky to Jonathan Haidt have argued for a smartphone-free classroom, recently I have started to use them regularly for review lessons in the form of Kahoot quizzes, which are fun and attention-grabbing and offer fine review structure. However, once we are through Kahooting, my students put their phones away, without being asked, and look to their old sage here for our next tasks that are not infrequently on paper.

All of my current students have smartphones, and some even try to write papers on them occasionally; however, they seem comfortable enough rele-gating their phones to private usages, at least while in my classroom, and taking up older platforms such as Microsoft Word and even paper and pen, both easy and reliable assignment delivery media. In "Confronting the Myth of the Digital Native," Megan O'Neil describes "a picture not of an army of app-building, HTML-typing twenty-somethings, but of a stratified landscape in which some, mostly privileged, young people use their skills constructively, while others lack even basic Internet knowledge" (*Chronicle* April 2014). O'Neil illuminates here a class dimension of the technology push, in my experience and observation one overlooked by administrations doing the pushing. Kentaro Toyamo sensitively develops this class challenge in the techno-boom's wake, in his to-the-point "Why Technology Will Never Fix Education" (*Chronicle* May 2015). In my experience, technology can too often add an extra layer of frustration and demand of time as we try to do simple assignments in class. How much time have we wasted trying to get the less-tech-savvy, and this certainly includes the instructor here, as well as those who cannot bring a laptop to our regular classroom, onto some trendy new cyber platform? How many of us have just wanted to abandon ship and go apply for a Walmart greeter position, anything but try to help students retrieve their passwords? There just isn't enough Xanax at that Walmart pharmacy, trust me.

I am not here to answer the useless question of whether the internet is good for learning, although I believe that this is a valid concern for humanists since we like all questions of epistemology, and many of us still believe that tools used for learning must be just that: servants of learning itself. However, this master-servant model might no longer work for us. I am here to overview some serious concerns that educators have, or should have, about the infant Digital Age and especially about what we as educators are being asked to swallow, not to mention do about and with "technology" in our practice. Foundational questions...

Under ever-increasing pressure to introduce more and more technology into our teaching, are we really being driven by the exigencies of better learning? This is certainly a question for humanist interrogation, given several related concerns. I propose three fronts for today's discussion: politics, practice, and promise—that promise we humanists want to uphold for our students, that is. I agree with Neil Postman, who as early as 1969, argued that it is the educator's task to protect our students' right to learning—not just "information" and job skills, but also how best to adapt, live, and thrive in their still-human world with all of its unquantifiable complexities and non-data-driven random challenges. He especially recommends that educators treat media as a primary and meta-cognitive curriculum: "...[W]e suggest that media study become an integral part of all your classes. No matter what 'subject' you are teaching, media are relevant" (Teaching 204; see especially chapter 13, "Strategies for Survival"). If we understand "media" not only as mass communication forms but also as the technologies taking over our classrooms and departments, I will proceed with warnings but conclude with some constructive recommendations.

Technology and Capitalism

Warning #1 will be no surprise to today's educators: the collusion between technology and late capitalism. Borrowing from Fredric Jameson's theory in his 1991 work, *Postmodernism, or the Cultural Logic of Late Capitalism*, I use "late capitalism" to describe a system in which all global systems are organized, if not unified, under the profit motive. Profit becomes the only valid consideration, and "progress" a function of maximizing it above all other, shall we say, more humanistic considerations. We could veer off now into a daylong coverage of capitalism's assault on higher education, transacted on various fronts: standardized testing, the lionization of STEM disciplines; Kevin Carey's current economics-based assault on the traditional universities (he calls them, scornfully metaphorizing their putative archaism, "cathedrals of knowledge"); the push to convert universities into vocational schools; and the "fall of the faculty," as Benjamin Ginsburg describes the replacement of education with profit-driven administration (who suck up a great deal of these profits at the expense of providing their students with full-time, well-compensated faculty); the student-loan bubble and the consequent purging of any academic aspirations outside of job training—and much more.

Institutions and educators feel continuous pressure to innovate, update, and expand technology-based learning; think of hybrid and "flipped" classrooms, MOOCs, and online proliferation in general, along with the threat to faculty jobs and salaries posed by mass-education forums that do not rely on physical presence, classrooms, utilities, experienced and knowledgeable instructors, and other costly elements of face-to-face instruction (see Kevin Carey for a hypertrophied explanation of this threat). "At its most pragmatic, digital humanities has less to do with ways of thinking than with problems of university administration," asserts Adam Kirsch in his piece, "Technology is Taking Over English Departments." Ever prodded by the profiteering technology industry and fiscally prudent administrations, educators can lose sight of the critical question: is all this technology really helping us teach and learn better? Information technology gives us, for sure, three things: faster speed, greater access, and improved data aggregation. How do these facilitate the kinds of learning that humanists in particular rely on and encourage? Does the digital revolution give us new ways to think and create—or only new ways to collect and catalogue what we know? And now, we witness and try to cope with the onslaught of AI and its corporate creators/sponsors reaching their tentacles into the very brains of our students. Creepy Barbie has grown up and become much creepier, not to mention omnipresent.

What do we know? Neil Postman addressed the problems of conflating scientific and humanistic methodologies; both are valid inquiries, but dollars come with data, not philosophizing. As Kirsch insists, "The humanities cannot take place in seconds" any more than they can thrive in the ecstasy of aggregated data gleaned from "everywhere, at once," unchanneled by the critical processes often unfriendly to Big Data.

Humanists might also engage with more dystopian speculations about our technopoly. As data-driven approaches increasingly dominate education, so does the demand for "efficiency," as non-educator legislators and administrators seek to make policy profitable. (In fact, the three most common buzzwords of the AI invasion are "efficiency," "automation," and "innovative"—how can the fascinatingly flawed human and centuries of tradition thrive within this unholy tech trinity?) Aldous Huxley articulated this concern in the Preface to *Brave New World* seventy years ago, stating, "in an age of advanced technology, inefficiency is the sin against the Holy Ghost." He argues that for the sake of efficiency and thus intensified and faster data-driving, technopoly slaves must love their enslavement, and "to make them love it is the task assigned...to ministries of propaganda, newspaper editors, and schoolteachers." The mass access, saturation, and speed available through technology can reach, engage, and inform more students than ever before—but at the potential cost of sacrificing intellectual rigor and redefining education as an instrument of capitalist indoctrination, antithetical to the humanist devotion to skepticism and critical inquiry and analysis. Henri Giroux has pointed to a "full-fledged effort through the use of the pedagogical practices of various cultural apparatuses . . . the new media and digital modes of communication . . . to produce elements of the authoritarian personality while crushing as much as possible any form of collective dissent and struggle."

Along with the constant exposure to mindless and even toxic popular culture, Giroux argues that information technology functions as a "distraction and disimagination machine in which mass emotions are channeled towards an attraction for spectacles while suffocating all vestiges of the imagination, promoting the idea that any act of critical thinking is an act of stupidity and offering up the illusion of agency through gimmicks like voting on American Idol" (Interview)—or, say, the classroom clicker, or voting in a presidential election.

I am reminded of one of my favorite Dystopia course lessons, on the *Black Mirror* episode "Fifteen Million Merits." Young people are enslaved in an apparent hi-tech prison, forced to pedal stationary bikes all day to power the vast system, which seems to have no external reality, nothing natural. Aside from the trite virtual kicks their avatars can experience (such as 24/7 pornography that you must pay to turn off!), their only relief is in the form of an American Idol-type competition, a spot-on parody of the real deal. The hero's struggle and ultimate coup of dissent are both upheld and subverted in a brilliant ironic twist and in the way of late capitalism: crush all dissent and revolution by commodifying it and making it profitable. I am no spoiler, so tune in on Netflix. As I say throughout here, you've just got to love much about the internet. Satan knew exactly what he was doing when he brought it to us.

Technology and the Learner

Lewis Lapham, in his introduction to Marshall McLuhan's iconic 1964 *Understanding Media: The Extensions of Man*, points to the basic kinship between writing and the technologies that convey it. Comparing print and electronic writing, McLuhan half-condemns, half-embraces the "sovereignty of the moment" promised by electric media, which ultimately "ends subjects in the world of learning" (346). We can see the fulfillment of his prophecy in the turn toward community and collaboration, and the ecstasy of Every-thing-Everywhere-at-once that digital literacy affords and even demands. Student "engagement" can no longer simply mean a student engaging with their own mind's processes and creations of their own mind; these must be "shared" in "small groups" in so-called collaborative classroom activities. I once had an evaluator ding me because only about eighteen out of twenty-five students spoke up in the class session that day. "How can you know they are learning anything?" he insisted. Does a student's sitting in reflective silence during class, not blurting out whatever comes to their head in order to meet their required contribution, mean they are not learning anything? What about the quality of those contributors' insights? That consideration did not seem to matter. What of the quality of the contributor's offerings? That didn't seem to matter. "Everyone has to contribute during class." This isn't teaching and learning; it's a form of data driving, and you can't data-drive silent reflection. Also, in a class meeting of fifty minutes, if twenty-five students contribute—and let's allow at least two minutes for each contri-bution since just speaking does not constitute a viable contribution; there must be audience reflection and response—well, that takes up the whole class period. Where's the instructor or the instruction in all this? There's only everyone giving their opinion in an ominous reflection of life online.

In a higher education economy increasingly hostile to the individual, either as sage-on-the-stage instructor or silent, allegedly non-"engaged" learner we might closely consider the end of the learning subject. With the panopticon potential and lightning speed of the internet, are our learners to be blended into the ecstasy of everywhere, at the expense of their individual autonomy? Kevin Carey certainly thinks so within his utopian vision of a world of uniformly (in spite of his learning-style hype) prepared, able, and avid cyber-learners out there, ready to acquire MIT-level knowledge with just their laptops and WiFi. Sherry Turkle points to psychological hurdles online, observing that "we fill our days with ongoing connection, denying ourselves time to think and dream," and warns of the hollow payoff of "simu-lation: the exhilaration of creativity without its pressures, the excitement of exploration without its risks" (224). I would call this an apt description of the everybody-must-speak rule of the contemporary classroom. In simula-tion, the gamer or surfer actually occupies a new identity, presumably one superior to the awkward biological mind and body so prone to error and underachievement in Real Life (see Mark Slouka for an early history and analysis of cyber life vs. "RL"). Our human students, required under penalty of point loss, must pop out their daily Pez pellet of class contribution and thus feed that hour's data aggregate.

A strange irony emerges in digital-literate culture: the have-it-your-way mentality of everything today from MickeyD's to the classroom. Dan Tapscott, author of *The Eight Net Gen Norms*, observes that "Young people insist on freedom of choice. It's a basic feature of their media diet...The search for freedom is transforming education as well. Learning for them should take place where and when they want it" (132). They will no longer accept the role of passive vessel to a sage-on-the-stage dictator. In fact, the very idea that such a sage could have anything valuable to say has been pretty much discredited; never mind that the experts doing this discrediting were largely informed and trained, via print literacy, by such sages. But Logan LaPlante, the "hackschool" superstar with his charming narratives of his 13-year-old experience and obvious ethnic and socioeconomic status indicators, has ruled the world of TED-talk pedagogy lite ever since, devoured by higher ed. However unknowingly channeling Wordsworth and Whitman (whom he might not ever stumble across in his online freestyling), he tells his young audience to flee the traditional classroom and creatively explore the vast Everywhere with their pricey technology and Starbucks internet hookup.

What will this confident young autodidact eventually give the world? We hope for a better Picasso, a more complex Joyce, a perfect vaccine for all COVID strains, or a better mousetrap. Free of the onerous constraints of informed direction, without tedious professional educator guidance, under his own creative auspices and with his trusty devices, he is the great hope of the digitized future. He might even succeed in quickly making himself obsolete, obviously a goal of the digitechnicons. For more on Logan's iconoclastic TED, see my later chapter on TEDs, and be prepared to hate—certainly not Logan, but me, who dares to question this smart and self-motivated youngster on his much-touted edutainment platform.

So why aren't my college kids OK? Why isn't everyone, everywhere, ecstatic? McLuhan prophesied the future, perhaps temporarily as an evolutionary stage but nonetheless currently ensnared in the intersection of, or our wandering between somewhere and everywhere. Nicholas Carr in his 2010 *The Shallows*, and many others since, write of the neuroscience of multitasking, and the news isn't good for our students' ability to reason clearly and argue effectively. Already we see our right to individual privacy, reflection, and autonomy—the hallmark of print culture with its solitary and self-engaged act of reading—eroded or even obliterated, as collateral damage to our self-expansion into collective consciousness. (The majority of my students today either admit to "not reading" or apologetically say, "Well, I read social media postings, memes, stuff about my video game," and so on. However wearily, I reassure them that these are valid texts today for their scant reading time.) McLuhan had predicted the anxieties that plague our classrooms as well as our society at large. Could these anxieties be inevitable to the "electric circus"? Our students, raised on TV as we were but also the Internet, cannot "take refuge in the zombie trance" of print linearity and detachment; thus, they and their instructors panic as "we all become Chicken Littles, scurrying around frantically in search of our former identities, and in the process unleash tremendous violence. As the preliterate confronts the literate in the post-literate arena, as new information patterns inundate and uproot the old, mental breakdowns of varying degrees—including the collective nervous breakdowns of whole societies unable to resolve their crises of identity—will become very common" (Playboy interview 126). Any honest instructor today will admit to moments, if not semesters, of such panic if not breakdown.

What Is the Thing Called Technology?

The following reflections come with hope because educators are very good at this kind of hope. We must attend to our students' "terrible anxieties" while optimizing their learning experience in the Divide. Sherry Turkle has argued what we know so well, "We have to find a way to live with seductive technology and make it work for our purposes. This is hard and will take work" (294). Her sentence has recently become all the more imperative as we stare down the new presence of AI ChatGPT, which I call Professor Alexa, that can research and write any paper for free and almost instantly, and which doomsayers promise to be "the death of college," or at least the essay. Apocalyptic thinking aside, Turkle is cautiously optimistic, believing that "When we are at our best, thinking about technology brings us back to questions about what really matters" (294-95). Some contemporary optimists believe this applies to the new ChatGPT, claiming that it's a call for instructors to learn how to work constructively with this iconoclastic cheat technology, incorporating it into a legitimate learning experience in our classrooms. Now that's a tall order—within our current Stockholm-Syndrome confusion, how to turn plagiarism into scholarship, a painful smashup of opposites. We have arrived at technology that can free students from the onerous drudgery of their own thinking, research, analysis, evaluation, and creation. Perhaps soon, we instructors will have an AI teaching assistant who "grades" these assembly-line assessments. Will we still get paid anything? (It has been opined that courses will still need an instructor as a sort of "facilitator" to troubleshoot, provide occasional meta-counsel, etc.) Will students learn anything? In digital heaven, a man's reach might exceed his grasp, but at the expense of his hand.

Note how Turkle echoes Martin Heidegger in his famous take on technology: "In this way we are already sojourning within the open space of destining, a destining that in no way confines us to a stultified compulsion to push on blindly with technology or, what comes to the same thing, to rebel helplessly against it and curse it as the work of the devil" (The Question 25). ChatGPT might well be the work of the devil, but apparently we instructors must make peace with it; and making peace with the devil has ever been a tricky and risky business.

I am especially attracted to Heidegger's most careful definition of what "technology" fundamentally is. Not the latest invention by Apple or the latest online Cengage lab—nor TED talk, YouTube, TikTok, Google, ChatGPT, nor whatever latest commodity fad. "Technology is a means to an end...[and] a human activity. These two definitions of technology belong together. For to posit ends and procure and utilize them is a human activity." For him, technology is a means for humans to draw from what he calls the "standing-reserve" of "world" and to shape, "unlock, transform, store and distribute" the standing-reserve of phenomena. These are some of the "ways of revealing," and it can be no surprise that "this revealing never comes to an end." Heidegger delivers a strong message about our relationship to technology as educational practice, where a retooling of traditional practice can respond to the call of new phenomena.

We must adopt a meta-pedagogy of technology in our classrooms. That is, we must always perform the metacognitive act of calling our students' attention to both the definitions and the non-instrumental implications of the technologies they use. To avoid or evade this is not only to shut off one of the rich pathways of revealing their being-in-the-world, but also to create great individual and cultural danger for them: Heidegger explains that "we shall never experience our relationship to the essence of technology so long as we merely conceive and push forward the technological, put up with it, or evade it. Everywhere we remain unfree and chained to technology, whether we passionately affirm or deny it. But we are delivered over to it in the worst possible way when we regard it as something neutral" (4). It is my claim that "the worst possible way" appears in the classroom where technology is imposed by cultural and administrative fiat, without the requirement of self-reflection, critical inquiry, and metacognitive practice—not to mention consciousness of and conscience about unethical behavior.

"What is clear is that, to date, computer technology has served to strengthen Technopoly's hold, making people believe that technological innovation is synonymous with human progress" (Postman "*Technopoly*"). Nowhere is this more evident today than in education. A collusion of seductive market forces, state funding requirements, cultural lapses, eroded literacy, a school-closing pandemic (driving everyone online), and the demands of globalism has frightened educators into grasping at short-term solutions mostly involving technology. We have tended to fall short of, or even fear, asking critical questions about not only what technology does but even what it is. We still insist on thinking of it as our tool, not the other way around, as proposed by David Skrbina and others who believe the tide has turned, and not in human favor. We do not see that some, if not most, of the changes in our practice derive from the demands of the digital medium, and these might not be the best for our students, not only in their learning but also in their human thriving. Yes, the pandemic brought on some mild questioning, based on our students' evident suffering while forced online; however, there must be much more broad and deep questioning now and ongoing.

Technology is indeed an amazing tool that we bring in to supplement our human instruction. However, as I have indicated here, there is a menacing telos within the technology push, one that bodes ill for the physical classroom and human instructors who, after all, tend to be expensive and relatively inefficient by algorithmic standards. At this time, we will not look into how the techno-utopists plan to wean humankind from its eternal profit-seeking addiction, to the point where the University of Everywhere is as freely provided, both in availability and cost, to the world as promised, satisfying demands for inclusion, equity, and access. Much lip service is paid to these needs without much understanding of how they can be fulfilled, especially when it comes to AI.

Within the deluge and push of technology, we want to avoid "selling our birthright for a mess of apps," insists Adam Kirsch. It is likely the humanists among us who will insist on fighting this fight for our birthright, which is to keep the human element strong in education. In spite of what profiteering education technology, state legislators, budget-conscious administrators, and starry-eyed technophile instructors want to believe—our students are still human and seem to strongly prefer, not to mention succeed in, face-to-face classes with their human contact, support, and personal mentoring. They do love their devices for social media, which is a great use for these.

These can even be brought productively into play in metacognitive assign-ments in which students wrestle with not only the subject at hand but also how technology supports both learning the field and practicing it nowa-days. But everyone needs to keep a close eye on how these media and devices constitute a radical reshaping of our world, a paradigm shift unparalleled since the printing press, and also on the fact that the advantages these tech-nologies bring are calculable in terms of efficiency, the totalitarian state's first mover, according to Orwell and Huxley, and even more ominously, cost-cutting and bottom-line profit.

Two decades ago, Ira Shor defined "critical literacy" as "learning to read and write as part of the process of becoming conscious of one's experience as historically constructed within specific power relations" (Anderson and Irvine 82 qtd. in Shor). I am arguing today that it is the humanist educator's challenge and responsibility, not to say destiny, to interrogate these power relations, remedy an unhealthy neutrality about technology's promise, stave off the worst encroachments of the voracious market, and most of all, bring our students as aware critical thinkers into the argument.

Chapter 3: The Divide Conquers: Presence and Absence Onsite and Online

> Teacher, leave them kids alone.
>
> —Pink Floyd

> To let the child do as he likes when he has not yet developed any power of control is to betray the idea of freedom.
>
> —Maria Montessori

In his introduction to a hilariously empirical study of American social class, simply entitled *Class*, Paul Fussell observes that when he tells people the subject of his new book, "It is as if I had said I am working on a book urging the beating to death of baby whales using the bodies of dead baby seals." Such is the taboo of the topic, the incredulity of the reader, the impossibility of the claim that America actually has a class structure. Well, prepare yourselves for some pearl-clutching as I intend to throw shade on not only online education but also TED Talks.

First, please understand that I make appreciative and beneficial use of both. I teach online, which I have liked much more than I thought I would. Against my inclinations, I took a training course and started teaching online for some classes about ten years ago. I did this because I thought I would hate it and find it to be the cold, alienating, soulless platform of my dystopian paranoia; feeling this way, I knew I had to try it and see for myself. To my surprise, I enjoyed learning a new skill set and trying it out with my students, who adapted well enough. In short, I had few of the problems I expected and experienced some unexpected victories, such as a greater overall participation in the course along with my ability (albeit out of necessity) to communicate more closely with more of my students in writing through their assignments, emails, and in chat room and Zoom sessions. I believe this requirement for more extensive written communication (via comments on papers, discussion boards, email, etc.) has brought me closer to a few more of my students than the classroom allows, given the quick comings and goings before and after class, plus human shyness and reticence before the physical *eminence grise* of the professor (or just the social-media-induced reticence to speak face-to-face with another human being). Also, it cannot be rationally denied that the online platform can bring education more readily to more students, especially nowadays with the insane schedules that too many young people must maintain to earn income, raise a family, tend to their elderly and unwell, and more. Online education makes education available everywhere, to everyone with a computer and the tuition fees, and that must be a good thing.

There are protests about the proliferation of online diploma mills serving up diminished quality undergraduate and relatively useless graduate degrees in both nonprofit and for-profit setups. However, I feel neither inclined nor qualified to talk about these here. As a lifelong guardian of effective education, I understand such concerns and hope questions are always asked, especially by the students who seek and receive degrees from these institutions.

A few preliminary words are necessary about my reasoning behind this chapter and the next. I could simply tell you that I wanted a chance to vent before a larger audience than my captive classes, my suspicions about online learning, and my annoyance with the chosen TED Talks of the next chapter. This I will certainly do, as you shall soon see. However, I must place this venting into the larger context of perhaps my favorite lessons with my reading and writing students: argumentation and rhetoric. By these, I specifically mean the Logical Fallacies and the principal Rhetorical Devices. Logical fallacies are claims that have specific errors in reasoning and are thought to weaken the claim and even spotlight the utterer's ignorance. As for the latter charge, we can observe that the best and brightest indulge freely in logical fallacies as is witnessed in any political debate. Although it is challenging to teach all of this to my students, we nonetheless have lively sessions where I ask them to find logical fallacies and explain why these claims are illogical or unreasonable. I especially enjoy doing this with TED Talks, for reasons to be explored in the next chapter.

I have a second reason for cobbling together these critiques. I believe that the U.S., and I am told by my international students, the whole world, is making war on education—that is, education as I have known, loved, and practiced it. Everywhere we see the fundamental principles and truths of education subsumed and mutated by neoliberal logic; in short, in a world where profit is the chief goal (with entertainment a close second), what chance and place does learning for learning's sake have? Combine this *cui bono* logic with the Enlightenment ideal of the autonomous individual, imagining their "rights" and insisting on their right to follow their own star: "You do YOU!" Stir in a bit of Wordsworth, still an insidious Romantic hangover after all these years/centuries, and you complete the conditions for an ever-spreading web of fallacy:

> Our birth is but a sleep and a forgetting:
> The Soul that rises with us, our life's Star,
> Hath had elsewhere its setting
> And cometh from afar:
> Not in entire forgetfulness,
> And not in utter nakedness,
> But trailing clouds of glory do we come
> From God, who is our home:
> Heaven lies about us in our infancy!
> Shades of the prison-house begin to close
> Upon the growing Boy...

It is very heaven to be a child until the child must go to school and learn something from someone older, wiser, more experienced. That schoolhouse is a prison, and its trained and devoted teacher is a tyrant warden! How dare we treat kids this way?

Piqued exaggeration aside, what do I mean by all of this so far? I'm not fully sure myself since I have lifelong loved being in the classroom and devoting myself, assisted first by my teachers and then by my students, to learning new things, and I will do so till the end; thus, the process is always incomplete, reaching, growing, discovering, THINKING about the world and others in it. But I can focus specifically on Frederick Douglass, one of my American heroes. Douglass said, "Education means emancipation. It means light and liberty. It means the uplifting of the soul of man into the glorious light of truth, the light by which men can only be made free" (Blessings of Liberty and Education). For Douglass, education was the sole reliable and permanent path to freedom, and his narrative tells near-miraculous stories of how he went about, laboriously and over years, often at peril and through trickery, learning to read and write from the free white people in his life. This was the only way since it was illegal to educate a slave in literacy. A fully literate, critical thinker is still the greatest danger to slavery in all forms, hence the war against education here today.

I once kicked a whole class out over Frederick Douglass. My class of thirty-some college American Lit students had apparently refused to read about fifteen pages of Douglass' *Narrative* over the week's time we had between class meetings. When I asked them why they hadn't read the assignment, they claimed: "Too much, too boring, couldn't follow it, had to work, had personal issues," and so on. Too much! Too boring! I was livid. I said to them, "You drive up here in your SUVs, pull out your Macs, clutch your iPhones, surf your social media—and you don't care about your most precious possession of all: the right, ability, and opportunity to become educated. You have me up here, caring about you, working hard for you, and devoting myself to making sure you all get this possession. Whereas a poor enslaved boy had to risk his life and go to extraordinary effort to get letters of the alphabet from the kids on the street." They glared at me. A few, bored, checked their phones. "GET OUT— the sight of you disgusts me!" I stood there, glaring until they had all left the room. This was, for the instructor, unexpected and out of character; you had better believe they had done the reading, likely twice, for the next class meeting. I strongly suspect that however important and fascinating Douglass' narrative is for me, whatever was on their phones was far more interesting for them. At least, their cyber addictions had wired their minds against the ability to sustain interest for fifteen whole pages of print.

Next time, I could provide an audio of it; however, it still would demand fifteen whole minutes of attention, so... Little did I know that this unfortunate class meeting predicted a tidal wave of threat to my and Douglass' respect for education as the opportunity of having devoted teachers, vetted knowledge, and learning for the sake of a rich mental life, not to mention our very freedom. Simply put, this threat comes in dual and even contradictory goals: education "to get a job" and education as a utopian vision of self-gratification. And while both have been around for decades, if not centuries, their exponential strengthening and potential for finishing off education in the old model have been largely facilitated by Satan's weapon, the Internet.

Maybe you think the old model should be finished off; if you do, you're in great company. Libraries of studies target problems with education as I grew up with it. And the undercurrent of my entire study here is that times change, and we must change for these times. But we don't have to like it, and we old guard can just retire and die, I guess. Peter Serdyukov opens his "A Growing Formalization of Contemporary Online Education" with this blazing prediction: "Online learning (OL), or E-learning, has been steadily growing in the last 25 years. But the unprecedented global coronavirus pandemic initiated the biggest distance learning experiment in history. Since 2020, OL is spreading like brush fire across all types and levels of education. Online and automated learning modes as two converging trends of technology-based education are gaining momentum, and there is no doubt they will continue to grow. One day they will unquestionably merge and produce a completely automated virtual environment based on Artificial Intelligence (AI)".

And why not? Teachers, facilities, services, amenities, and grounds are all, first and foremost in neoliberal culture, expensive to maintain. Education without teachers? I'm already seeing it without students as ChatGPT takes over much of their role, increasingly. Before this, though, some of us can do well to consider what has brought us to this point, to return to foundational thinking and focus on some examples of changes in our education models, just to see what kind of (un)reason—and whose (dis)interest—these changes reflect and represent. This discussion is not meant to suggest that we throw away our laptops and go back a century, back to the little red schoolhouse. It is just meant to, as we do in our classes, generate some good constructive analysis and evaluation. And take some well-deserved swipes at logical fallacies coming at us from some who should know better, and some who aren't old enough to know better. Let's start with some critical angles on online education.

One Laptop Per Child—Negroponte's "Blurry Vision"

In a podcast asking the best questions about a famous failed project involving online education, MIT's "One Laptop Per Child," Jeffrey Young (2019) asks: What makes up a charismatic technology? A charismatic technology generally promises to do something really transformative in the world. It promises to make us all better people and to completely transform our lives. Ironically, though, it often makes those promises by referring to things that are already familiar to us. And this is something that charismatic leaders rely on, too. They echo our own values in some way. And so a charismatic technology similarly promises this quick fix transformation that is very common in the tech world. And in doing so, it echoes some of our existing values and sometimes some problematic values.

Studies abound on the positives and negatives of online learning, and these are valid on both sides. But I will say that to be against online learning is dangerously backward and narrow-minded. This is like being against progress. Also, how could we not appreciate online learning? Here's a way to expand access to education across the globe, during pandemic shut-ins, and locally to those with mobility, transportation, and any other obstacles to showing up for class. So I could never claim that online learning is Satan's work although it does use his tool/weapon, the internet and that we should abandon it as an inferior forum. Personally, with old age, road rage, and other challenges to commuting, I might just depend entirely on online teaching to continue my life's work and passion and be grateful for the technology that allows me to teach until, well, I shouldn't or can't anymore. That will be a sad day indeed for me.

Yet, for all this, we can still ask some serious questions about what moving online has done to education. One need attend to nothing more than the current wailing and gnashing of teeth over our students' learning losses and emotional deterioration over the 2019-21 pandemic time spent on the online classroom screen. This complex problem remains in the news; it took the pandemic to bring to a head and demand attention to the general downslide of American education over the past couple of decades. To stick to the phenomenon itself and in the general spirit of my study here, we shall examine some sensible specific critiques of the damage potential to online learning. This topic is big, and our time together is short, so our inquiry must remain focused and limited.

Cyber-Save the World!

"In 2005, MIT professor Nicholas Negroponte unveiled an idea so innovative that it had the potential of improving the lives of millions of people in developing countries around the world—a $100 laptop," writes Boston U. sophomore Namank Shah in "A Blurry Vision: Reconsidering the Failure of the One Laptop Per Child Initiative." Thus Shah launches his detailed breakdown of the "spectacular failure" of the One Laptop Per Child Initiative. OLPC's guru, Negroponte, lords it around the TED stage (2015), making claims so far-fetched that one has doubts about what's happening at MIT English departments. For one example, he claims that kids in developing countries don't leave school because they have to work or are needed at home; it's that "school is boring, not relevant," superimposing our Western bad habit of being "bored" on third-world children. Unable to resist what would become the rallying buzz-phrase of 21st pedagogy, he actually says that there was no "child-centric" learning in those places. In his new digitally enhanced spaces, kids are not subjected to the "horrible" pedagogies of "rote learning," "singing," and so on. He shows images of a dozen remote village seven-year-olds clustered around one laptop, mesmerized, as their parents "hang in through the classroom windows" to marvel at this and presumably see the need to cede their parental authority to their young techno-autodidacts.

The gods must indeed be crazy! Truancy ceases! Discipline problems disappear! This laptop does everything but serve school lunch to the kids (which might just be the most needed thing). It even can turn itself into an e-book, which due to the obvious intrinsic failure of the book medium, even in e-form, its inventor deems "a bit boring." Oh, that b-word. He gleefully recounts a story of a teacher who filed for early retirement because she didn't want to deal with the new laptops at her village school; however, they got delivered before her last day, and immediately addicted, she ended up filing for late retirement. One of her pupils did her homework, a project about cows, by filming her family's cow giving birth; this video was subsequently uploaded to YouTube, received 100,000 hits and "greatly boosted her esteem." I don't know about you, but watching a cow give birth is way down my list of leisure viewings; I'll take Netflix and Lifetime, thank you. But how wonderful for that simple village child, raised to near-influencer status by her benefactor OLPC.

Alas, as Shah's phrase above, "spectacular failure," indicates, things didn't continue so rosily for OLPC. The project proved doomed by both economic and cultural obstacles. The costs to manufacture the laptops almost doubled, from $100 to $180 per unit. More significantly, Shah argues that cultural insensitivity and blindness—that often, however unintentionally, accompany imperialist-colonialist projects—ensured that the project ultimately "failed to meet its idealistic expectations". OLPC in its first avatar did not tend to match the host cultures' visions and expectations, not to mention needs. (Apparently, these cultures did not yet value the need to go viral and raise one's self-esteem through cyber-celebrityhood.) Shah also points to the potential harm in "the rise of curiosity in the children" which could lead to conflict with parents as well as the raising of material expectations beyond the culture's ability, short- or long-term, to gratify. Nor would there be reason to gratify them since these expectations have grown from "the forcing of Western ideas on children in developing nations". In a world that sees the spread of English as lingua franca as a form of imperialism, how could OLPC be seen as anything less? How would world nations more grounded in local concerns and, well, their own reality deal with the image products of a nation (here, the U.S.) that, to paraphrase Jean Baudrillard, projects the id directly onto the material?

Last week, I had my international students do a presentation in which they chose a favorite song, played it, and analyzed it by the typical pop culture parameters. Almost all of them did this with a YouTube video for their song. One student from a Western nation popped up a video from his favorite singer, who he claimed would be singing about life in his nation's slums where, if this video is to be believed, the residents go about mostly or totally naked, twerking and performing various public sex acts. (Please understand that I do not think that this is how people in underprivileged, underserved communities really live; the video is a simulacrum of the maker's own desires for the audience.) I sat, horrified, watching some heads lower and most classmates generally turn various shades of embarrassed. A sort of jagged steam emanated from the class. My presenter, unfazed, continued his merry way through a reasonable analysis as his instructor tried to unfreeze herself and stop the porno show in her English classroom. Now, granted, they all had submitted their presentations before class for me to review for issues. Mea culpa, I hadn't gotten around to it. I hope I have learned from this, but back in the days when we submitted an essay or read one from the podium as our presentation, we wouldn't have to XXX-rate our lessons. Oh, and fortunately, I didn't get fired; however, if I hadn't had such an overall good rapport with my students, this would've been possible, for sure. One disgruntled member could have filmed the lot, and I wouldn't have taught in this or any other town again. In fact, not all cultures react to the same information in the same ways.

Shah admits that he doesn't want to "dismiss" the laptop project and constructively summarizes a remediation path. "Careful analysis about the culture and necessities of the children needs to be done in the countries." To drive home his true intention here, he continues: "the OLPC initiative can improve its success rate by letting go of its Western ideals and adapting its laptops to the appropriate needs of the children who are using them in developing countries" (89-90). Of course, this would add a herculean workload to the project, requiring careful study of each culture to identify all relevant factors. This would necessitate personnel in anthropological roles, not to mention teams of sociologists, psychologists, linguistic experts, religious guides, and much more. It would require spending some money, deeply cutting into the profits that MIT claims not to have made. It's much cheaper when you just need your high-tech first-world lab and your own cultural ideals. To study and honor the needs of others can require thinking outside one's own world and worldview. You'd imagine that such an esteemed institution and scholar would have been well aware of that from the get-go. I imagine that everyone involved was knowledgeable of such challenges, but the lure of the tech takeover, along with whatever non-profit benefits it might bring, proved strong enough to eclipse common sense.

I want to thank Namank Shah, who wrote this article as a sophomore at another esteemed university, Boston University, for his early recognition of the important requirements for real and respectful success in the global business arena, and for explaining everything so clearly. I wonder if he taught himself through a TikTok video how to write so well? I'd love to know.

Being Present, or All We Really Want

"I want to challenge you to look up...look for another human being. And know that what you're looking for isn't found in your pocket, it's inside them, and maybe inside you," closes teenaged Henry Williams in his TED Talk, *Alone, Together: How Technology Separates Us* (2018). Yes, this is a teenager in a TED Talk, but young Henry, in his poignant rhetoric, has surely hit on something valuable here.

For my second look at problems with online learning, I am choosing an article that, like Shah's case, crafts a line of argument clearly and persuasively. Bob Samuels published "Being Present—A Critique of Online Education" in January 2013, *avant le déluge*, which means before the mule had already gotten out of the gate, and education everywhere stormed online. As Serdyukov reminds us in 2021, there would be no stopping online education from growing larger, more pervasive, seductive, and then downright necessary in the pandemic years. I admire Samuels' long, strategically developed argument grounded in one claim: that we humans need to be with each other, in physical proximity and presence, and that this is our true first and foremost need in life. From this foundational claim, he traces the ways this need gets abandoned in online learning.

This is an excellent article for a "round-table read-in" with students, many of whom hold somewhat negative opinions of online learning while acknowledging the practical advantages it brings: cheaper, no commuting, no packing or buying lunches, no wardrobe expenses (though we all agree one must always wear some kind of pants while Zooming), no gas and other vehicle upkeep expenses, can be at home with kids (that has its disadvantages as well) and more. As I have mentioned, I enjoy online learning, providing and receiving, and am glad to have added it to my well-equipped and ever-expanding pedagogic toolbox. However much we might practice and profit from online learning, it is still worthwhile to take a critical look at where and how it can harm or fail us in our current human avatar. Two of Samuels' core tenets reflect my own in this study: the first is that moving online can be, for institutions, mainly about money and control; and relatedly, the second is making expensive and cumbersome faculty obsolete. This connects with Negroponte's (however misled) "child-centric" focus, Serdyukov's prediction, and my own critique of "student-centered" learning. My fear is that this last appears as a wolf-in-sheep's-clothing, inevitable to the first; we can sideline and eventually eliminate the faculty member. We are on our way to doing just this by a short list of powerful strategies: sideline, overwhelm, underpay.

If you want to save money in your institution, a good place to start is to shed both faculty and brick-and-mortar facilities with their accompanying maintenance bills, and move everyone to the virtual classroom, where you can pack the infinite "room" with many more students who will be taught by the same one instructor, drawing the same pay for the same work: planning, evaluating, grading, justifying, persuading, and placating—not the twenty-five that will fit in the physical classroom, but possibly even fifty or more. (A responsible institution will still reasonably cap its online classes; however, this is not guaranteed.) A small liberal-arts college told a job candidate that due to their popularity, more and more online classes would be added, some with a cap of sixty, and this is in a course requiring a lot of writing assignments. In such a crush, teaching and learning quality cannot help but suffer significantly as the instructor struggles to survive, too often literally.

Samuel sets out to "defend high-quality in-person classes" as essential to good higher education. He believes that lowering the quality of in-person classes by continually increasing their class size "equates university education with its worst forms of instruction, which will in turn open the door for distance learning." This happens because large class size necessarily reduces the personal engagement potential between instructor and student, classmate and classmate; and if this occurs, why not just move everything online, which is always already "highly impersonal and ineffective" in Samuels' opinion? This could be done primarily with the introductory courses, which arguably need the most personal and effective contact among their members. Although I do not agree that online education must necessarily be highly impersonal and ineffective, Samuels astutely argues how the potential for this is unquestionably increased in virtual classrooms for reasons that follow.

Another challenge to the large class is how to make such a class student-centered. Before online learning or even the internet took over higher education, back in the 1990s, I taught a literature class with 125 students in an auditorium-styled classroom. Although I am assured by student-centering devotees that it is possible to "get in small groups" and "flip the classroom" (another playful fantasy) even with such large numbers, I recall feeling restricted at that time, with the instructor-centered and now *verboten* lecture delivery model. We didn't even have PowerPoint back then. When I asked my chairman how I was to assign the usual 3-4 papers, involving critical analysis of the assigned readings, to a class of 125, he immediately said, "You don't." We were to have multiple-choice tests, and he gave me a teaching assistant to help me grade them. Now we can put all of these students online and have the learning platform and even AI grade them! Not only grade, but teach, tutor, and even "mentor": each student can have their own algorithmic assistant! What was overwhelming and exhausting to the human instructor wouldn't faze a robotic one.

Let us return to Samuels's concerns about the collateral damage of such a utopian vision for academic profiteering. He develops this argument line by pointing to the relative ease with which students can become "invisible" in online classes; it is harder to hide your full body and voice in the onsite classroom. He argues that online students can become alienated from physical presence, including human eye contact and body language, and teleologically from the physical environment and the natural world. Getting students fully acclimated to virtual life is required in the final solution for costly traditional education.

Alienation from the lesson focus also occurs as it is much easier to multitask while already online; the instructor cannot make you put away your technology (as if they could in any case) as you are actively learning on it. "When students have to be in a class and listen to their teacher and fellow learners, they are forced to turn off their cell phones and focus on a shared experience without the constant need to check their Facebook pages or latest texts." Although I have witnessed massive "multitasking" during my physical classes, I have also had students tell me that they welcome the enforced break from their techno-connectedness, even though I have never enforced this. I have never had a no-phone policy. They just seemed to come to this realization themselves: this is my break, where I can relax and focus on one real thing right in my stable physical space. Now, I have taught both asynchronous (no virtual class meeting) and synchronous (scheduled class meeting where you must show up on screen) classes; I must say that synchronous does help mitigate this problem, as students must show up on screen and provide evidence of participating in the class. In fact, sometimes this participation is superior to that attempted in the physical environment. As for asynchronous classes, I could have no idea what they were doing while working on the course; however, their work quality overall seemed about on par with synchronous and classroom learning.

Samuels insists that online learning caters to "a libertarian ideology that tells [students] that only the individual matters, and there is no such thing as a public space anymore." This is closely tied to "edutainment," which serves to "sell the new generation of students short by arguing that they can only learn if they are being entertained or if learning is an exciting, self-paced activity." Three decades ago, Neil Postman, in his chapter "Teaching as an Amusing Activity," had the extreme gumption to attack *Sesame Street* as the foundational text for all of this (*Amusing Ourselves* 142-54). In 2013 Logan LaPlante, who likely nursed his child's brain on *Sesame Street*, believed that all he needed is "my laptop and a Starbucks" to educate himself. However, his true goal is "to be happy," a necessarily subjective state shut down by the rigors of public education.

I myself have had to adjust to continuously brainstorming "engaging" lesson activities for my adult students; pedagogy today seems to long for 100% "student-centered" lessons. My problem with the phrase "student-centered" education is simply, when was it not? Does anyone really think that all educators in the past were there to educate themselves in the "instructor-centered" classroom? Talk about a logical fallacy, Hasty Generalization or Dicto Simpliciter, at least. A colleague once stopped by my classroom soon after class started and blurted out, "Why are the desks like this?" They were still in auditorium style as I was showing the class a video, about which we would do various exercises. The idea was that they should already be in circles, pairs, cornrows, mazes, starbursts—anything but the archaic, boring, traditional classroom furniture arrangement. I have been advised, "You have to get them up and moving around." We are talking about college students here, many of whom are in their thirties and forties. Why moving around? First, someone has to move the chairs around. Second, because it's obviously too much to ask an adult learner to sit for an hour. They should be walking around or sitting in the "small groups" chatting with each other, teaching each other and themselves ("I don't pay tuition to learn from the idiot sitting next to me," growled one student)—anything but listening to the boring old instructor droning on from the podium. "Yet, we still need to teach people to concentrate and sustain their attention when things may get a little boring or difficult," insists Samuels. He obviously thinks about what will happen when all these restless autodidacts go to med or law school or even just get a real job, all situations not necessarily offering a me-centered, amusing frolic in class or office.

Samuels clings to print-literate models and outdated notions of authority when he says, "students need to be taught by expert educators about how to access, analyze, criticize, synthesize, and communicate knowledge from multiple perspectives and disciplines," which he seems to believe must be done (or at least best done) in the physical classroom. I cannot fully agree that online learning must make this so much more difficult. I do agree that online learning opens loopholes or even escape hatches from such linear and laborious intellectual processes. We have all seen our students grab their phones when asked a question. I once assigned them to draft a personal narrative about a valuable experience they had; fifteen minutes later, they were still surfing their screens. "What are you doing? You're supposed to be writing a personal narrative." "We are looking up 'personal narrative,'" they explained. They didn't trust my explanation of this genre and had to ask Google. Samuels' anxiety here leads him to his ultimate paranoia: being out of a job.

"The web also creates the illusion that all information is available and accessible to anyone at any time. This common view represses the real disparities of access in our world and also undermines the need for educational experts. After all, if you can get all knowledge from Wikipedia or a Google search, why do you need teachers or even colleges?" His "disparities of access" plagued the OLPC initiative and continues to exist as the common "digital divide," where some have full and easy access to machine learning and others just can't afford it or have no community support for it. As for his latter claim, this is the greater danger by far. No less than David Hume, father of modern Western philosophy, argued that humans never act first from reason alone: all actions are first motivated by "passion," or feelings about how this act will benefit me. Like Samuels, I have a passion for paying mortgage and eating and thus want to keep my job; perhaps unlike him, I turned to online learning a decade ago, believing that even when the tired old sage-on-the-stage finally gets the boot, they will still need someone to grade papers in online courses. At least I hope that machines will never be assigned this task; human grading can be onerous, but any other way truly will topple the whole project of education or at least change its MO exclusively to impersonal and efficient data aggregation.

Samuels aligns this threat in online education with the already-well-criticized proliferation of dependence on adjunct contingent faculty, who are overworked, underpaid and taken heartless advantage of by business-model higher education. "Student-centered education" becomes for him a red herring, distracting us from the dismantling of responsible education: "In the rhetoric of student-centered education, the teacher is reduced to being a 'guide on the side,' and this downgraded position entails that there is no need to give this facilitator tenure or a stable position . . . and so it is little wonder that colleges operating only online employ most of their faculty off the tenure track." This is a fact at the major online universities today. Classes at these institutions tend to come "course-in-a-box," where the instructor is mainly part of a stable of rubric-wielding graders and has little control over curriculum, methodology and assessment. The professor becomes a glorified clerk, wearily burning midnight oil, eyes straining to mark rubrics for hundreds of submissions, many if not most at least partially plagiarized. Socrates (or at least Plato) must be spinning in his grave.

I have attended training sessions required of new online adjuncts. My most recent training, in my professional estimation, was first class; the institution planned it, in both humanity and technology, enviably. We were kindly and carefully, not to mention helpfully supervised by expert colleagues. I was so pleased at how much I learned about the current ways of online learning and teaching. This is both challenging and refreshing, as I feel like a student navigating new territory scared and excited, and forced to swim or sink. Such instructor experiences make us more empathetic toward our students.

There is, however, one aspect that I find deeply troubling. In the profession at large, we have watched our class experience co-opted by outside forces. By "outside," I mean anyone outside of the instructor herself, along with the department chair and dean as needed (and this very occasionally). But as learning has continued to be moved, from the physical classroom, chalkboard and textbook to online platforms we see our practice as increasingly surveilled and monitored, not to mention dictated by someone other than the instructor. This points back to Samuel's justified paranoia, that the instructor is fading out of usefulness. In fact, although there is much rhetoric about our "contributing from our experience and expertise" to course pedagogy, there really isn't a lot of room for that, and I perceive that we are glorified graders, a stable of data providers for the institution that claims that such a system is in the student's best interest. After all, doesn't data fix everything, so the more the better? This is "accountability" in the extreme, on all levels: instructor, administrative staff, and institution itself. For the first two, I can understand the accountability. But the last? To whom is the institution itself accountable? Well, full circle back to the students, for one. If they aren't satisfied—for example they get a poor grade or don't pass the course—there goes the income. It boils down to *cui bono* after all. Of course, we all want to believe that this "bono" is the student's, who passes everything, gets her degree and goes on to a great future. So why not celebrate the data-driving machine if it keeps everyone accountable, helps students and economically fuels the institution? Well, because we've all lived through the great stink about standardized testing in K-12 and the great profiteering permitted of outside business forces in public schools. Somehow, this kumbaya accountability circle has greedy tentacles reaching into it from the business sector.

My second trouble in the new dictated, monitored, and surveilled curriculum—possible mainly due to being online—keeps me up at night. The issue is not only that I have increasingly, over the past couple of decades, lost control of my lesson content with the push for curriculum standardization.

My greater concern is this: as an English instructor, I have my students share a great deal of their thoughts and life experiences with me, and I have always considered this a special privilege to be guarded at any cost, as a physician and lawyer must do with their patients and clients. It would be the height of unethical behavior to share a student's thoughts and stories, not to mention grades and progress, with anyone else. The old idea was that as an instructor, I was to be trusted to teach, monitor, and evaluate my students and then share the results in the form of grades, with those eligible to see them: the student, parents if K-12, and the institution itself. Beyond these, the student must solicit and approve sharing this information, say with future colleges, professional schools, and employers.

Now, learning online in an institution where every keystroke on the learning platform can be monitored, presumably for the altruistic reason of ensuring our students' maximum success, where has privacy gone? Everything they do, write as an assignment, and communicate to me personally can be surveilled and responded to by those other than me, the instructor. We are even told that if we see disturbing things in our students' writing, we should refer them, by email, to various college services including mental health. As I mentioned above, my English composition students are asked, in various types of assignments, to share so much about their personal and professional lives, their families, their hopes and dreams, their beliefs and opinions, their mistakes and disappointments, their preferences, and so on. How is their doing this in the new surveillance state that is online learning so different from the perils of oversharing on social media? What is to prevent an institution (I speak generally here) from selling this information to outside data miners for profit? While I must believe that this is not only unethical but also illegal—not to mention dystopian—is it that far out of possibility? Wherever data is gathered, it is stored, and who can guarantee protection from its being shared with forces who should have no rights to this as they have no responsibility for the student's education?

Henry Giroux prophesied this danger, predicting a global war of not only capitalism but also authoritarianism (he got that right): "this 'hard war' against the American people will be supplemented by a 'soft war' produced with the aid of new electronic technologies of surveillance and control, but there will also be a full-fledged effort through the use of the pedagogical practices of various cultural apparatuses, extending from the schools and the older forms of media . . . to the new media and digital modes of communication . . . crushing as much as possible any form of collective dissent and struggle" (Truthout). Online and even today on the omnipresent learning platforms used in onsite instruction as well, I do not feel comfortable asking my students to write about topics that have been common fruitful ones for us. And I so much want to tell them all, in my first posting to them, "You have absolutely no privacy here." But since that would be surveilled, and I would be dismissed, and I want to remain there for them, I forbear.

I would love to feel assured that this mass surveillance of my students doesn't and cannot happen. But I've lived in this capitalist economy too long and with the coming of the internet, witnessed the massive potential, both sanctioned and criminal, of using data to deceive, bilk and harm those who provide it. All I can say at this point is, prove me wrong. I won't hold my breath.

Now, let's turn in the next chapter from clubbing baby whales to torturing baby seals: our TED Talk critique. Let's just say I'm doing it here because I can, and it's a fun critical analysis effort for both me and my students. This past week, I used at least four TEDs in my classes, where we practiced listening skills, note-taking, summary, argumentation, and critical analysis using this form of text-source. We had a good time with these TEDs. Who wouldn't? You spend 10-15 minutes tops with a dynamic speaker, some compelling visuals on the PowerPoint behind them, and an ooh-aahing audience. Plus, you get a neatly dispensed pellet of ABCD (Already Been Chewed and Digested) argument. As a bonus, this pellet is life-changing and maybe even paradigm-shifting! For the English class bent on quickly learning argumentation, the TED Talk is a multivitamin, delivering in one pill a whole lesson on literacy and life, not to mention an easy hour's class activity. The TED Talk is one upgrade from the Power Point, which my students claim is too-often misused: they've reported that too many of their instructors simply light up and click through power-pointed notes, without discussion or deviation into critical inquiry. Instructors at podiums lecturing in their human voices, from their notes on paper, is now forbidden, practically deserving a disciplinary hearing; however, serving this same lecture by pointing at the overcrowded slides of a Power Point is somehow OK, I suppose since it's an electronic medium, a screen. It's more like watching TV—it's got visuals— than just listening to a person droning on in the obviously archaic and useless lecture mode. Need we once again acknowledge that most of these new "facilitators" in the "flipped" classroom were, themselves, educated by the sage-on-the-stage model? These experts who got smart enough to know how bad and wrong lecture class is, got to this expertise largely by means of lecture classes? Should they now be discredited due to their faulty education? I mean, isn't it ironic.

Chapter 4: TEDucation—Re-mixing Knowledge Through Pez-Pellet Information and Utopian Rhetoric

> Our politics, religion, news, athletics, education, and commerce have been transformed into congenial adjuncts of show business, largely without protest or even much popular notice. The result is that we are a people on the verge of amusing ourselves to death.

—Neil Postman

Who wouldn't love TED Talks? My students and I enjoy and profit from TEDs. They might be knowledge fast food, but they are tasty and fast, the primary desideratum created and satisfied by the internet. With their more serious academic credentials (many Talkers are already famous; most presenters take on a professorial air), they can lord it over most of YouTube and of course, due to the very nature of the medium, TikTok. Not to criticize here YouTube and TikTok; my students now tell me that they get most of their information from these two. The message is that the last source you want to offer students now is lecturing from your yellowed lecture notes or a textbook, which is overwhelmingly verbal, prohibitively expensive and nowadays likely outdated one hour after its publication, not to mention tl;dr. Not to mention likely culture biased and historically inaccurate. So we take in a lot of TEDs, not to mention YouTubes and TikToks and any other information source that makes things faster and simpler for us. And you see, that's the root of the problem: the internet makes it possible for everything we do, seek, try, work for to be for us, about us and reduced, compressed, simplified. We must make do with the information in the echo chamber because the reliable contextual glue of knowledge is increasingly dissolved. Who needs it as long as I get just what I want, and fast?

Those who have been privy to my sniping at TEDs tell me that I'm missing their point: it's a venue for speakers to come and present a talk about their area of interest and expertise. The very acronym speaks to their original intention of Technology, Entertainment, Design and their place in the new mission of fusing these three, conceived around the same time that Postman was prophesying this new "edutainment" medium. A cursory over-view of their history reveals the repeated charge to "change the world," and in fifteen minutes, no less. This is all bold and exciting, and it really isn't the TED phenomenon itself that is my target here. My target is how we, as an academic culture, have adapted to this mode of "learning" represented by the fifteen minutes of fame. My students have sighed to me, "All we do now is watch TEDs and talk about them." I remind them, "Yeah, and we're doing that here in my class, too." We do this not to learn how to change the world; rather, we are studying how to construct a pretty much entirely fallacious argument and still get fifteen minutes of fame.

What follows here is a close analysis of three of my area's most popular TEDs, the ones that I regularly assign as a critical analysis and evaluation lesson:

1. School is deadly: Sir Ken Robinson, "Do Schools Kill Creativity?" (2007)
2. School is unhappy: Logan LaPlante, "Hackschooling Makes Me Happy" (2013)
3. School is useless: Eddy Zhong, "How School Makes Kids Less Intelligent" (2015)

What we do here is some standard interrogation of logical fallacy along with some rhetorical analysis: ethos, logos, pathos. This is what my classes and I do with these, and trust me, you'll get farther with this TED form of text than with Aristotle, Kant, or Russell. When I perceived that my students couldn't, or at least wouldn't, read even fifteen pages from *The Narrative of the Life of Frederick Douglass* for the sake of logical and rhetorical analysis, I sensed that the old world was dying and that I must blunder into the new. Fortunately, TED was there to welcome me, along with fast knowledge and argumentation-lesson snacks.

1. School is Deadly, so why not just dance?—Sir Ken Robinson

In 2006, esteemed U.K. education theorist and professor Sir Ken Robinson gave what is touted as "the most popular TED Talk of all time," posing the menacing question, "Do Schools Kill Creativity?" Among my three chosen TED talkers, Sir Ken is undoubtedly highly credentialed, experienced, and competent to take the stage and share his insights. With a strong background in researching, teaching, and supporting arts education, he is certainly worth twenty minutes of our attention. He is also witty and charming, with a winning stage presence, rhetorical virtuosity and that appealing British accent. So, why in the world would academic Karen here call the manager on such a formidable presence?

I am not alone in my suspicions about the ultimate practicality, if not the truth value of Robinson's claims. Tim Leunig, equally officially credentialed, gave a counterargument in his own 2016 TED entitled "Why Real Creativity is Based on Knowledge." "Real creativity, successful creativity, world-changing creativity is based on knowledge. Our schools are equipping our children with knowledge so they can be properly creative." His own claim implies that Sir Ken's must hold that "creativity" is a sort of God-given, sui generis capability inherent in each of us that can be stifled and even "killed" by the socially driven structures of formal education. Both arguments represent parts of the whole elephant that is "creativity," which, by its very definition, cannot be entirely embraced, specifically defined, or even well understood. This nature-vs.-nurture debate, characteristic of a long history of education theory, will go on. What I find interesting in Sir Ken's take, is the predominance of abstract ideas and logical fallacies—pleasing to hear but not so much to apply. And Unlike Logan and Eddy, his two teenaged successors that I will discuss here, he is older and highly educated (in the same system he attacks, I will add) and experienced enough to know better.

After a spate of witticisms and wisecracks, Robinson offers a foundational argument, that "nobody has a clue what the world will look like in five years' time, and yet we're meant to be educating [students] for it." Aside from the Fallacy of Anonymous Authority—that "nobody"—this is simply untrue. Although the world is changing rapidly, it doesn't morph from one discrete form to another, moment by moment. I believe that we do definitely "have a clue" about what the world will look like in the near and even distant future because this world will, as ever, build on the existing world, about which we do know some things. I am reminded of Thomas Kuhn's *The Structure of Scientific Revolution*, where he argues that scientific achievement is not a long, gradual unfolding of truth but rather occurs as disruptions based on someone's almost-intuitive perceived "anomalies" in existing established theory, something amiss that strikes the right scientist and ultimately brings about a paradigm shift in that theory. But this intuitive perceiver, with their flash of genius recognition, comes to this point via a thorough training in the established theory. Otherwise, how would they know that there was anything to be concerned about? I do not believe that Sir Ken really thinks that intuitive types create revolutions in a vacuum; yet, his general-audience-appeal rhetoric, that flippant "we don't have a clue," would suggest that possibly he could. Robinson's next point is "all kids have tremendous talents, and we squander them ruthlessly." All of us, ruthlessly. With the Anonymous Authority attributions and hyperbolic adverb, I feel like I'm reading one of my own freshman essays. He supports this claim with an anecdote about a quiet, distracted little girl in art class who told her teacher that she was drawing a picture of God. But the teacher countered, "no one knows what God looks like." "They will in a minute," the girl replies. This cute story covers the ugly truth proposed by Sir Ken: that this teacher, if she had her way, would keep us from seeing what God looks like. We must be very grateful that the little girl insisted on her right to illustrate her divine insight.

"If you're not prepared to be wrong, you'll never come up with anything original." On this, he is surely correct. However, he follows with "and by the time they get to be adults, most kids have lost that capacity." Has he really been able to survey "most kids" to discover that all of these cannot come up with anything original? How did he do that: track "most kids" throughout their education and then measure their capacity to be original? Did he do this in his native England, or in the West, or globally? "We're now running national education systems where mistakes are the worst things you can make." If you buy this so far, you will buy his next grand generalization that "we are educating people out of their creative capacities." He cites Picasso, who claimed that "all children are born artists," but "we get educated out of it." Vast, vague, and unsupportable claims indeed.

Apparently, for Sir Ken, being a traditional educator, especially a professor, is the opposite of being an artist. "You'd have to conclude that the whole purpose of public education throughout the world is to produce university professors." After reminding us that he "used to be one," meaning I suppose that he escaped those stifling clutches, so we can trust him, he says, "we shouldn't hold [professors] up as the high-water mark of all human achievement. They're just another form of life." But they are a curious sort of life form that "live in their heads...They're disembodied, you know, in a kind of literal way." Literal? Wow. This composite of fallacious claims and diction lapses takes him to his next joke, the not-entirely-inaccurate "their bodies are just a means of transport to take their heads to meetings." This is quickly followed by a stereotype of Ph.D.'s as terrible dancers. What a pathetic animal, or at least mediocre at best, having wasted a lifetime of study and application of their study as Robinson himself had done before he followed the divine light leading him to TED celebrityhood.

You recall Bob Samuels' valid paranoia, that we are trying to get rid of the expensive "present" faculty, de trop in a world where students can educate themselves online and in their small groups and community amuse- ments, which themselves are necessary as there can be no more lecture-style learning by these mediocre disembodied heads floating behind the podium. You must find some way to spend class time, after all. While Robinson does not specifically point to online education or the internet, these have become the tools of an intellectual economy that increasingly devalues presence and authority. I include him here because he reflects the insidious theoretical foundation of death to public, in-person education. At least here, he gives tasty fodder to those untrained in or incapable of formal logic and inclined to suspicion about what happens at schools, especially if they didn't spend much quality time in any.

Robinson does mention "technology and its transformational effect on work" as the next step in his takedown of university education, especially. (We might again mention AI large-language models such as ChatGPT, a technology that is greatly transforming work, especially the academic kind and much for the worse, as I have previously known and respected it and according to current experts, "more and more of these tools will be integrated into the learning environment.") Although this statement sort of dangles in his argument, I believe that he uses it to launch his next missile. After arguing that the whole purpose of education seems to be preparing students for university, he claims that thus, "degrees aren't worth anything. Isn't that true?" Because technology is increasingly taking over certain processes of work, any university degree a student gets must be worthless? Within the whole context of their lives and not just for a specific job at a given moment? At this point, I can only pray that he later reviewed his undergrad notes in logic and felt a pang of regret. Except that having devalued his professors who taught him such as logic, maybe he doesn't now, in a burst of ironic intuition, see the need for avoiding vast, unsupportable generalizations about such a complex phenomenon as education and the impact of it on students' futures.

I must mention his final supporting example for the failure if not lethality of school, his evocation of Gillian Lynne, the dancer who choreographed *Cats*. Bored, distracted, and fidgety at school, the child Gillian was sent to a canny therapist who quickly recognized that "she's not bored—she's a dancer," explaining why she couldn't behave properly in school when he witnessed her responding to music while in his office. Her schoolteachers, trying to manage a whole populous English or math classroom, had made the egregious mistake of not recognizing that one of their charges was to become a professional dancer and choreographer. She didn't have ADHD, he says, because "that wasn't invented yet, you couldn't have that yet." (Along with this swipe at ADHD, he insults his wife's cooking and women in general making one wonder how this talk(er) survived at all into the twenty-teens.) One of my side-gigs as a disembodied mediocre head was to site-visit twenty-five elementary school classrooms and evaluate the teachers. What I witnessed in these visits assures me that no teacher should be required to sacrifice classroom order for the sake of one individual's budding genius. Not only is this logically absurd—if everyone is a budding genius, as per Robinson's claim, then really no one is—but never mind, you cannot teach anything but dance in a roomful of dancing children. Not only this, but teachers do perceive and encourage budding genius every day, every class. This just must be done in a way that satisfies federal, state, local, and school requirements for curriculum and testing for large groups of students at all levels. And while such a system certainly warrants some change, hence the outcry against standardized testing, for good reasons, how would a revolutionized education system look? Can it happen overnight? "Our education has mined our minds in the way that we strip-mine the earth for a particular commodity." This tortured metaphor and hyperbolic accusation supports his concluding claim that we must do nothing short of "adopt a new conception of human ecology," yes, no less than "nothing short," and one that demands that we "reconstitute our conception of human capacity," especially the imagination, and learn to "teach the whole being." Noble indeed but how, how long, and to what practical end? And just what is this "whole being"? Are we speaking ontologically or epistemologically?

Sir Ken passed away in 2020, which disallows my fantasy to talk with him about how he feels about turning education over to the machines, AI, and the cyber-hive, which must call for new conceptions of "creativity" as something profoundly NOT personal and individual. Perhaps this, too, is a fallacy-damaged claim. If education is to be turned entirely over to the cyber lords' spaces and economies, we educators, however resistant, cannot just abandon ship. I fully agree with Robinson's concluding claim about our students, "We may not see this future, but they will. And our job is to help them make something of it." This is the educator's ultimate purpose and will be the focus of my final chapters, the requisite glimmer of hope or at least a plan of action, as Technopoly ever expands its armies and invades the temple.

School is Unhappy, so let's all go skiing—Logan LaPlante

Now for some inexcusable tormenting of an especially adorable baby whale: Logan LaPlante. In 2013, Logan, at age thirteen, gave another of TED's most globally popular talks, "Hackschooling Makes Me Happy." In this talk, he practically single-handedly revolutionized education, lending a tremendous eleven minutes' validation to the growing practice of homeschooling. His parents, for reasons he does not divulge, took him out of school at the age of nine. From that point, Logan "hacked" his education, apparently by surfing the net, finding community opportunities, and learning what he liked, what "stoked" him, and made him happy. The "hacker mindset" leads him to not use any one curriculum or approach, but to "hack" his own personal education. "I'm not afraid to look for shortcuts or hacks to get a better, faster result." There's that "faster," in my world never a goal of education. He pulls out the jargon, "It's like a remix or a mashup of learning." Not sure what is being remixed and mashed up, but it sounds very techno-cutting-edge, doesn't it? Also, "the hacker mindset can change the world," bringing in that requisite charge of the TED talker. Logan's talk remains an emblem of the effort to tear down an oppressive, suppressive public school system and release its inmates into a more creative, healthier, and happier form of world-changing education.

I forget how I first came across Logan's TED (surfing around online, no doubt), but it quickly became a staple in teaching argumentation and rhetoric in my Composition classes. This talk would always capture and hold my students' attention and attract them into lively discussion. After all, who wouldn't love this handsome, plucky youth who "just wants to be happy?" I admire Logan and am grateful to him for providing this engaging text. Since research has shown that increasingly over the past decade, students do not read and must be assigned videos for analysis work, a good one is a pearl of great pedagogic price.

However, even homeschooling superstar Logan cannot escape some important critical questions, ones that tie him in with Ken Robinson's own tragic flaw. Logan often evokes Ken in his talk and is frequently paired with Ken in the ongoing marketing of homeschooling as an alternative to the creativity-and-happiness-killing traditional public school system. These questions are: how can you ground such an ultimately successful argument in a utopian generalization? Relatedly, how does this argument hold up when we consider what my students and I call "the thrilling three": race, class, and gender? These inquiries are thrilling because they will always provide us with something to talk about, for most any text. We might also look back to MIT's One Laptop Per Child initiative, as Logan claims that his laptop is essentially all he needs for his education. Oh, and a seat at Starbucks. Let's take a closer look at his argument and critique it gently.

He starts by claiming that when adults ask kids what they want to be when they grow up, they get the wrong answers. Adults expect answers like "astronaut," he says, but kids will typically reply with "something they're stoked on, what we think is cool, what we have experience with. This is often the opposite of what adults want to hear." While this may be true in some instances, is it true for all adults? He makes a very specific claim, "the opposite of," within the vast set of "adults." He continues by stating that if you ask a little kid, that kid will answer, "I just want to be happy." Storybook stuff, really, but when we consider how famous this claim has made Logan, we have questions.

"Go to school, go to college, get a job, get married, then you'll be happy, right?" Again, he assumes that adults monolithically preach this pathway. He is accurate in that this pathway might be hegemonic, or even a post-industrial capitalist pipeline to the status quo bourgeois. But the problem is that the system disrupts its own pathway: "But we don't seem to be making how to be happy and healthy a priority in our schools. It's separate from schools." When I first heard this one, I thought, "My time in school made me happy and healthy, so I don't agree." But specific counterpoints aren't admitted here. Logan argues that for some kids, this pathway doesn't work at all, and I'm sure he's right about that. However, these two claims: that school's primary aim should be towards a subjective and even culturally relative goal like being happy, and that anyway, this goal is "separate from school," falter on logical as well as practical grounds. Ask a Chinese or Japanese student, as I have had many occasions to do, if their schooling primarily aimed to make them "happy," and you'll get an uncomprehending stare. This "school should make kids happy" seems to be at the least, a Fallacy of Exclusion, where evidence important to the argument's outcome is excluded. What are the other contexts and purposes of schooling? And how might these not align with or even be counter to "happiness," which really is subjective anyway— especially when you take into account the Thrilling Three.

Logan offers a slide showing some good Logos in eight factors impacting happiness: "exercise, diet & nutrition, time in nature, contribution & service, relationships, recreation, relaxation & stress mgt. [sic], religious & spiritual." Dr. Roger Walsh, the author of these factors, believes that schools are not trying to impart these "Therapeutic Life Changes or TLCs" and are instead focused on teaching kids how to "make a living instead of making a life." Although undoubtedly a valid breakdown of components contributing to happiness, the list is compromised by the real situations of too many American, and indeed global, kids (recall the spectacular failure of OLPC). Since Logan devotes most of the remainder of his talk to specific examples of how he himself pursued these strategies through his "hackschooling" life-style, it seems he believes these opportunities are available to all kids. When I ask my classes, which are predominantly composed of working-to-middle-class and nonwhite students, how they visualize Logan, they answer: white, rich, rich community, mom and dad together, great family, etc. I add that since he is also male, this eliminates some of barriers, for example access and safety (for example, in exploring woods, camping, or skiing remote slopes) that could impede achieving these goals.

This perspective becomes even more apparent when we consider other world cultures. When Logan asks, "Out of the 200 million who have watched Sir Ken Robinson's talk, why aren't there more kids like me out there?" it's worth considering that more kids may not fit the profile of being white, privileged, and supported by a strong family—not to mention being American and at least middle class. These TLCs require substantial money, time, opportunity, and support. Logan is fortunate to have all these advan-tages and makes a great argument on behalf of others like him, but what can the rest of kids do, who do not have these boons?

Logan's hackschooling is "flexible, opportunistic, and never loses sight of making happiness, health, and creativity a priority. Here's the cool part: it's a mindset, not a system." This mindset appears to be the individual's judgment of what he or she desires, bringing us back to the subjectivity of happiness. He states, "My teachers wanted me to write about butterflies and rainbows, and I wanted to write about skiing." Well, there we are, finally: heaven forbid students should have to sacrifice shortcuts, hacks, remixes, and mashups corresponding to their personal desires at any given moment, to master a subject using the traditional tools and pathways of schoolbook learning. He gleefully describes "hacking physics." Seriously? I have spent much of my adult life among physicists and scientists, and I wonder how far this TED would fly at a STEM conference. Physicists, computer scientists, physicians, engineers in my acquaintance have shed seas of blood, sweat and tears at schools, in the pursuit of their esteemed professions. Did this make them unhappy? This question highlights the potential flaw in Logan's entire argu-ment. Must the goals and purposes of education necessarily align with the pursuit of happiness? Maybe only in the echo chambers created by the internet's allure of fast, happiness-inducing hacking. To my students nodding and smiling approvingly at Logan's liberating rhetoric, I ask, "Would you really want your surgeon, or the engineer who built the bridge under your car, to have hacked their education?" This puts a hitch in their giddyup.

"If everyone skied this mountain the way most people think of education, everyone would be skiing the same line, probably the safest, and most of the powder would go untouched. I look at this and see a thousand possibilities." Aside from his conclusion reinforcing the vast hasty generalization web of his argument line, he reminds us that he grew up in Lake Tahoe, a wealthy resort community and has had apparently unlimited access to skiing, not a cheap sport. Logan hacks his education the way he skis: free, unfettered by tradition or convention, and supported by great privilege. Logan went on from there to return to high school eventually, for the social benefits, and at the age of twenty-three has already become an entrepreneur, public speaker, education consultant and competitive skier. He seems to be happy, and I applaud that.

My argument here is not intended to discredit Logan's skill as a thinker and presenter, as well as a thirteen-year-old with circumscribed privilege and limited world experience, can present in this understandably super-popular TED talk. My students love him and often choose him as the winner in our class debates about "the most successful argument" when comparing several TED talks. Rather, I use this TED to illustrate how this platform packages concise, easily digestible, and rhetorically pleasing truths—at least, someone's truths—in the pinnacle of contemporary edutainment. I am sorry that Neil Postman isn't here to witness us amusing ourselves to death while believing we are absorbing world-changing ideas. Do these ideas always hold up in the real world? As Postman's own guru Marshall McLuhan famously stated, the medium is the message, and TED gives us that message faster, hacked, remixed, and mashed up. And, it makes us happy. Shouldn't that be education's highest goal? If so, TED is indeed our best textbook.

School is Useless, So Let's All Start a Startup—Eddy Zhong

Often my students choose Eddy Zhong's nine-minute TED as their favorite among Sir Ken's, Logan's and his. They account him "more professional," appearing as he does in a dapper suit and with "more realistic evidence," as they perceive. He was sixteen years old at the time of his 2015 TED appearance, yet TED claims this about him: "Eddy Zhong, successful technology entrepreneur, dives into the truth behind our K-12 education system." Once again, we enter a Wordsworthian space where kids, evidently superior in knowledge and experience (which they drag blazing from heaven at their birth), can take the lead. Having become a successful entrepreneur by sixteen while managing his own big business, this charming young speaker is certainly impressive. Let's look at some specifics.

Rhetorically, Eddy opens by teasing us with his "big secret," one that we might find unappealing: "Every day kids go to school, they become less intelligent." One might be tempted to stop watching at that point, as this claim seems absurd, a fact he acknowledges and promises to clarify. He goes on to share that he was not good at school, claiming to be "the only Asian kid who's bad at math," leveraging this popular stereotype to reinforce his point. He also mentions that exercise was something he engaged in "every two years," and that he received no birthday party invitations. This is not surprising for a kid who aspired to be "a professional Call of Duty player" when he grew up; we can infer that he spent a considerable amount of time playing video games, a familiar profile for many of our students today. However, at age fourteen, he found his "salvation" and was "now like a supersonic jet flying toward my destination," no longer aimless due to his "useless" schooling. This salvation came in the form of a business plan competition, which he attended and subsequently launched his supersonic rise in the world.

Over the next two years, Eddy attended "dozens and dozens of these competitions, and I was winning almost all of them." This is admirable, no doubt. He then tells about how when he tried to pitch ideas and assemble a team at his high school, he was ignored and even mocked. But when he took his act to his elementary school, the little kids went crazy for it and were "throwing their lunch money" at him, trying to invest. The comparison is apt, and we can hear Wordsworth's ghost reciting:

> Shades of the prison-house begin to close
> Upon the growing Boy,
> But he beholds the light, and whence it flows,
> He sees it in his joy . . .
> At length the Man perceives it die away,
> And fade into the light of common day.

And what is responsible for this condemnation of youth, if not darkness, becoming "common"? Since Eddy has only two minutes left, he works fast: "And I think this is what our education has done. In just five or six years, these creative children have turned into teenagers that are unwilling to think outside the box."

Oh, how I have come to hate that box, dragged out on every occasion that someone wants to complain about how stifling, oppressive, restricting, and dulling that experience generally is. The fact that this "box" is rarely, if ever, clearly defined, and that other factors (the Fallacy of Exclusion rears its busy head again) are not referenced, like a person's own effort or motivation or the amount of money and support they might have access to, proves irrelevant as the box-shaming cliché is wielded. Like his contemporary Logan, Eddy charges a monolithic "school" with robbing kids of their "creative" intelligence by "teaching them to think a certain way, go down a certain path in life," predictably by teaching them the standard subjects dictated by a society that just wants you to go to more school, get degrees, get a job, etc. It turns out that these assertions, based on abstractions, are pretty much the only grounds he offers for his thesis: that school makes us less intelligent. How then do my students regularly judge him as offering the "most realistic support" for his claim?

This support comes in the form of one Hasty Generalization, described above, and one very specific example, himself. Here we sniff the Unrepresentative Sample fallacy, as Eddy clearly was and is gifted with natural smarts and a lot of pure hustle. This hustle is "what can't be measured with academic intelligence alone." I remain bothered by his association of passing school subjects such as math, history, and physics with "intelligence"; isn't this just knowledge, things you've learned? By my long experience and close observation, I consider students intelligent who take this subject knowledge and spin it into all kinds of graduate and professional study, careers, arts, and personal life fulfillment, using their "creative" minds in the alchemical shaping of knowledge into life. Not to mention that they also get jobs, which are useful for paying rent, buying food, and more. By cleanly prioritizing "creative" intelligence while separating it from all things academic, Eddy can shine the winner's spotlight even more brightly on himself, admittedly a C-student.

"You can open your own doors. You can stray away from this conventional, limited, and narrow path that education sets us upon." You can become an entrepreneur, like him! Why doesn't every kid just do this? Why doesn't every educator and parent open their eyes and influence kids toward the entrepreneurial path?

I personally would rather see more teachers, doctors, lawyers, engineers, business managers—not to mention mechanics, plumbers, electricians, carpenters, even computer scientists and technologists out there providing the materials and services we need to sustain society and individual life. Last I checked, these require a traditional educational background. If all kids "diverge and create [their] own future," surely a utopian one, what will happen to all us poor schlubs out here who need stuff and to get things made and repaired? Should we all drop what we're doing, forget our own stocks of knowledge derived from our schooling, and become entrepreneurs? Forget becoming a doctor to help patients heal and thrive; just find investors start a chain of medical clinics!

Eddy ends like he began, with a big secret: "no one has ever changed the world by doing what the world has told them to do." In terms of logic, what does this even mean? How can we define "what the world has told them to do"? He must mean what it told them to do in school, so we're back to that school-as-useless thing. There is no pill strong enough to cure this Romantic hangover we seem to have because audiences have loved Eddy's TED. And I love it too, but not for its teachable moment, which strikes me as full of logical holes, ill-defined concepts, and lack of any viable support beyond the speaker himself. I love it because Eddy has done so well for himself and gives most of us, apparently, a successful personal-example argument for his pathway. Mean English teacher aside for the moment, you can't help but love that for this bright young entrepreneur.

Now that you all hate me for beating up on two bright, beautiful kids and one of our time's most influential adult educators, I suppose I'd best just close this chapter. However, remember that my real target is not these powerful speakers but rather their vehicle: the medium as the message, the TED Talk. Marshall McLuhan and Neil Postman are grinning from their graves at our TED-worship, as in these we have fused education and entertainment, now pandemically offered as "edutainment." I will remind you that Neil Postman takes a big swipe at the iconic *Sesame Street*, to which he assigns the irony of being a foundational text of learning's fall from grace. Of course, we get some education, but it's the entertainment that deprives too many of the sense and legitimacy of argument derived from slow, painstaking scholarship: the method and goal of print literacy. But this is obviously the outdated opinion of someone whose creativity and imagination were crushed by their formal education. How did I get to this bogus place, and why am I still in it? Why do I not give up and just wander the streets, dragging my tired old box and pulling people down to pray with me about lost worlds?

OK, not entirely finished here. Let me tell you how I really feel. These TEDS attacked school, my temple, and threw some shade at my religion: education, as I have known and loved it. So if I have taken some hard swings at them, it's only fair. Don't anger your mean old English teacher because if you do, you'll get hit by a logical fallacy charge faster than you can say Post Hoc Ergo Propter Hoc.

CHAPTER 5: POLICE AND THIEVES — FOUR CLASSROOM CYBER CRIMES

> All the crimes committed, day by day
>
> No one tried to stop them, in any way
>
> All the peace makers turn war officers
>
> Hear what I say!
>
> —Junior Murvin, "Police and Thieves"

Perhaps the most foundational motivation I have had in producing this volume is academia's current frustration and despair over what to do about ChatGPT. A major conversation topic among my colleagues now is *what can we do*? (The dominant answer tends toward capitulation.) Has the internet finally dealt the death blow to human originality, creativity, and trust—not to mention ethics? When I recently submitted, on the counsel of my faculty mentor, a repeat Chat offender to our office of academic integrity, I was gaslit in a five-point message: in my accusation that I could not ground because Chat detection sites are not trustworthy, I had potentially harmed the student, tarnished the institution, brought the possibility of legal retaliation, failed to continue trying to work with the student in a "helpful" way, and my favorite, committed an ethical violation. In my view, the worst ethical violation is allowing this student to pass unscathed (since we apparently have no way to prove the violation outside, that is, of multiple AI detection sites, TurnItIn's own site, and my own four decades of evaluating student performance) with a high mark while honest classmates trudging through their own work could earn less and even fail the course. I have come to appreciate and welcome the worst my students can do because I can be pretty sure that they themselves did it.

This and the next chapter take up this ridiculous situation of those of us devoting our lives to teaching and learning, only to have been ever-increasingly challenged, threatened, frustrated, bamboozled, and overwhelmed by all the ways the internet has encouraged and facilitated academic dishonesty. Strangely, we can't, much less do anything about it, even seem to talk about it too much among ourselves. Hussin and Ismail (2013) have called plagiarism a "taboo" due to its pervasive evil and instructors' unwillingness even to think and especially to talk about it, both with each other and with supervisors, the main reason being the legal and "ethical" violations we risk attempting to deal with plagiarism. (One also suspects, following the argument of such as Jonathan Haidt and Greg Lukianoff's 2018 *The Coddling of the American Mind*, that accusations of academic dishonesty must become taboo since youth are permitted to think, feel and do whatever they wish without repercussion, out of fear of ignoring someone's learning style, committing microaggression, inducing trauma or PTSD, or simply making someone unhappy.)

We will have occasion to explore on a more scholarly level the new internet-borne academic dishonesty dystopia, but first let us enjoy some good stories. The following are four tales of academic dishonesty cyber-terror, spanning two decades. One is fiction, three are some version of reality. Names have been changed or omitted in a reluctant gesture to protect the guilty. I have a fantasy of instructors everywhere submitting their own tales of TurnItIn and Terror to a collection; however, this would threaten to overcrowd even the biggest libraries—if we're still talking about print libraries. But there is room for all in cyberspace, one of its ironically redeeming virtues.

The Case of the Terminal Trill

The Professor surveyed her pupils from the lofty situation of her podium. Her podium was, in fact, a pulpit since her class was scheduled to meet here in the university cathedral. How fitting for her, Great Books in the temple, a literal one.

This cathedral was of the Gothic persuasion, an immense stone monument replete with the characteristic arches, buttresses and gargoyles of its European forebears. Professor took in the ethereal heights and metaphysical glooms of the sanctuary's depths and pronounced them appropriate to her mission here: to communicate the majesty and power of knowledge to her eager charges. Opening the great tome before her, her eyes fell worshipfully on the words of Goethe; today the class was to feast upon the age-old legend of Faust, to witness the terrible wonder of a man's selling his soul to the devil for a taste of God's omniscience. Her eyes brimming, the Professor inhaled a meditative breath and began to recite the Prologue in Heaven.

"Brrrrrrrrrrrr"

The buzzy trill commandeered attention like a techno-pop music of the spheres. Everyone sucked in a collective breath and waited:

"Brrrrrrrrrrrr"

"What is that noise?" Professor queried, with some restraint, from her pulpit. A moment's hard silence, and then a voice followed the next ring.

"It's my cell phone." Professor directed a disbelieving gaze toward the confession. Goethe and—it was too horrible—a phone?

"Your cell phone is ringing in the middle of class?" Professor demanded the obvious.

"Do you have a problem with that?" The student brandished the phone as if to illustrate her point to the clueless teacher.

Expelling a resigned sigh, Professor reached under the pulpit and into her briefcase. She extracted the .38 Snubnose she always carried for just such emergencies, held it aloft, aimed it carefully and discharged it. The deafening report shook the stained glass of the Gothic structure. The .38's missile struck the offending instrument dead center, blowing it into a hundred plastic shards and wire bits.

"Not anymore," said the professor, puffing at the smoking barrel, then re-cocking the weapon. She re-aimed, this time at the dull gray area between the finally interested eyes of the former phone's owner, who had evidently failed to read the sentence in her syllabus about deactivating electronic equipment before class.

The Case of the Pole-Dancing Plagiarist

To start off, I assure you that I have nothing against "sex workers." That the main character here identified as a sex worker is beside the point, except for allowing a touch of irony at the tale's climax.

While teaching at the university, I suffered all kinds of slights and misfortunes. A whopper occurred when my Creative Writing course registration number was accidentally merged with my required Freshman Comp registration number. So I ended up with thirty students, maximum for the course; however, at least twenty of these had no business in a CW course: an opinion shared by both sides of the podium. But there was no remedy as these students needed the credit hours, it was too late to re-register, and after all, who cared? It was the ever-adaptable instructor's problem.

Most adjusted well enough to their new Comp I "creative" reality. In fact, by term's end, some had found new hope in self-expression. Most of them passed, honestly enough. But there was one memorable exception to the "honestly" and the "self-expression." This was Chrissy, who told me on the first day, in TMI detail, about her current job as a stripper in a popular local club. As I said at the start, no prejudice here; rather, when I learned what she made weekly and compared it to my own pathetic teacher salary, I envied her. I recalled that in grad school, in a Classical Greek seminar, I had a classmate who also worked as a stripper in a top local club. She was brilliant and gorgeous and made about a grand a week, working a couple of nights. Her translations of ancient Greek were solid. All in all, she impressed the hell out of me, and I have never forgotten nor stopped envying her. But back to my story.

A handsome lady with a killer bod, Chrissy immediately impressed the class and was always first to hop up and read her assignments. She loved to share stories about herself and wrote little ditties about stripping, fending off aggressive clients while stripping, and suffering the hardships of single motherhood. In retrospect, I can't be sure any of these were original, but they were engaging. She wore flimsy, short sundresses and had a low, smoky voice. Her presence at the podium seduced the class, all right.

I received her frequently in my office, where she told me way too much about her history of trauma, abuse, and degradation at the hands of family, men, friends, strangers, customers, and the occasional teacher. I have generally appreciated students' sharing their challenges with me, but something about Chrissy gave me pause. Yes, she was warm and personable, but there was something about her eyes... When I chanced to look into them, I recalled Coleridge's lines from "Christabel":

> A snake's small eye blinks dull and shy;
> And the lady's eyes they shrunk in her head,
> Each shrunk up to a serpent's eye
> ... with somewhat of malice, and more of dread.

A colleague hosted a big party in his backyard, adjacent to campus; and back then we were in the habit of inviting students to party with us. (How times have changed, most likely, in this case, for the better.) I had invited my Creative Writing class to come and by experience, if you invite thirty, maybe three will actually show up. Chrissy did. I was there with my then-boyfriend, a liaison about which she knew. (Our office visits did include some girl talk.) Later in the evening, I happened upon the BF and Chrissy, who was on him like a cheap suit, wrapped around him, arms and legs. And he did not seem to be resisting at all. When I entered the scene, with that deer-in-the-head-lights look, he gave her a sort of shove. She stumbled a bit, then looked at me, looked up at him—and bit her wineglass, crushing it with her teeth. He just stood there, staring stupidly at me. Since I had the car keys, I left the party.

Oddly perhaps, this scene was never mentioned between Chrissy and me. As we were approaching term's end, I thought it best to just drop my umbrage, at least against her, and focus on business. And I bet you are by now wondering, "What does this have to do with our overall theme here?" Read on and learn that it was worth waiting for. You see, Chrissy provided me the motivation finally to check out this new craze, the internet, and to learn, at first acquaintance, its potential for evil.

The CW students had a "capstone project," which they would present to the class the final week. They could prepare a collection or a single epic poem. Some even mounted photographs on poster board and wrote poetic captions beneath. One, an especially resentful and hostile victim of the registration mix-up, turned it to gold and composed a chapbook dedicated to his true love who, upon being presented with this unique original gift, accepted his marriage proposal. Candy is dandy, liquor is quicker, but poetry alone is a guarantee.

Chrissy naturally demanded to be the first presenter. Classmates had shared with me their projects in process, but I hadn't yet seen a word of hers; "You just wait, you'll love it." On presentation day one, I excitedly watched her assume the podium, multi-page manuscript in hand. The class, rapt, awaited her masterpiece. She began to read, with an appropriately rapturous tone, her offering titled *Did Jesus Use a Modem in the Sermon on the Mount?* Her ballad-style verse was metrically faultless, tightly rhymed, mature in form and diction, while conveying the unsurprising message that Jesus did not need electronic media for his goals and purposes—and long, around fifty lines or so. Although I was little acquainted with the language modem, RAM, joystick, PC, I got her message and thought the poem rather good. A splendid achievement, in fact, for someone who had, to date, opted for loose emo free-verse ramblings and submitted nothing in rhyme or meter of any footage. I also found it interesting that a self-proclaimed sex worker, in her grand finale, turned to a Christian theme. Irony, or atonement for perceived sin? So far with her, sin had never come into the conversation.

Chrissy delivered in a hushed but powerful tone the final wisdom, "Then set aside your laptop and modem/And all your fancy gear./And open your Bible, open your heart/And let your Father draw you near." I am using a current internet version; the poem has gotten around quite a bit since 1998, the time of this tale, and I no longer have Chrissy's submitted version. The class sat, also hushed, almost in tears. One student then exclaimed, "Well, then, never mind my pitiful effort here." "I know—I can't follow that!" "Chrissy, you are poetic genius!" I was happy for her; she deserved this affirmation and uplift; perhaps it would serve as healing to her traumatized past and fraught (recall the bitten glass) present. This could be a new start for her, grounded in her mental and spiritual rather than corporeal talents!

However, my hopes proved short lived.

When all had presented, and we had said our emotional goodbyes for the term, I was heading back to my office when a classmate solemnly approached me: "Dr. Sapp, can we talk? Chrissy didn't write that poem." Really? "Seriously, Doc, she didn't." How would you know? Isn't this the first time you've heard it? "Check the Worldwide Web."

Now, I did know about the WWW as I had a friend whose marriage had been destroyed in a "chat room." This alone had scared me away from it. Of course, I had used computers as fancy typewriters for basic word processing for some years already; also, I had been supplied a clunky PC for my office, but I had thus far ignored it. I saw no reason to complicate my life and add to my task burden with something mechanical. Mine was a quill-and-scroll world.

"Don't you know the internet?" Well, I know of it... "Here, let me show you..."

What followed shattered my trust, likely forever, in all that I had previously held sacred: creativity, originality, truth, beauty, the uniqueness of the human spirit and expression. In other words, my profession. My student tapped at the keys on my desk device, and boom, there it was, already "shared" a million times, *Did Jesus Have a Modem...* Translated into twenty languages, thus far. Oy veh!

The blow to my trust receded in importance before my resentment at what she had done to the class. Liar, cheat, thief—she had made them insecure about their own honest efforts. I had heard them defer, bowing and scraping before her poetic genius, presumably inspired by no less than J.C. Seething with rage, I composed a message to Chrissy. I can't recall how I delivered it because I am now incapable of imagining many things before the internet.

Chrissy did come to my office, and I confronted her with the crime. A zero on the capstone could result in a failing grade. (She had also missed some assignments due to "personal issues," which I had surely had to understand and wave aside with a "don't worry." These would now go in as zeroes.) She saw she was forced to confess to the plagiarism but played every card: poverty-stricken, overwhelmed single mom, manic-depressive, oppressed sex worker. I didn't tell her that I too had, in my time, been all of the above—in other words, "girlfriend" and "wife"—but worse since I had never received any compensation for my own forms of oppression. She cried and begged for forgiveness.

I did end up passing her, with a "C," but nonetheless a passing grade. My generosity got rewarded a year or so later when a student informed me of a conversation she had overheard in a ladies' room, at the graduation ceremony. Details about how this student knew the connection between Chrissy and me aside, the informant reported these of Chrissy's triumphant words from her stall: "I cheated my way through all of college."

Assisted, no doubt frequently, by my new worst enemy: the godforsaken internet. But as they say, if you can't beat 'em, join 'em. And join 'em I have been forced to as the whole academic industry is now reliant on the devil's weapon. And I must say, even as I wrote this, I have Googled not just a few things; however, I always give proper attribution. To do otherwise is thievery, and thou shalt not steal (*The Holy Bible*, Exodus 20:15).

The Case of the Sexting Schoolkids

Forever, I had taught in this program. Seriously, it had been seventeen years. This program was a summer thing, bringing high school kids from age fourteen to seventeen to our institution for a college-prep program. The goal was to prepare them for college, and they got automatic scholarship funding upon successfully completing the program. And as all of you in the business know, and I use the term "business" deliberately these days, it would have been in our best interest to allow as many students as ethically possible to complete the program.

At this point you may ask, why would a rational college instructor agree to the obvious potential torture of teaching academically at-risk high schoolers in a college-prep camp? Trust me, the salary stank, as they all do for such part-time gigs. So why? Why? Well, some of us loved working with these fresh and hopeful young minds and enjoyed their lively company. Some of us really wanted to make a difference! OK, some of us needed the summer salary, any way we could get it.

They spent five weeks with us, ensconced in dorms and following a brutal schedule from 7 a.m. (P.E. and then breakfast!) to 5 p.m. During this time, they would have four or five classes, each lasting sixty to seventy-five minutes, covering the gamut of English to Math, with various diversions to tangential curricula like Debate and Theater. Our campers were troopers, dedicated to our demands while making and enjoying new friendships. Honestly, it was a pleasure to be with them during those summers, Until it wasn't.

We didn't see it coming, but we recognized it when it arrived. Our kids became detached, bored, agitated, rebellious, and frankly obnoxious. This transformation occurred over a period of about three years. What had happened?

Yes, you know it, you are not wrong: they had all gotten smart phones. This had not happened suddenly—or had it? Due to behavioral devolutions in our charges, changes in program policy became demanded. Cruelty of cruelties, we did not allow them to keep their phones while in our program. They had to turn them in upon arrival and adjust themselves to doing without them for five whole weeks. Yeah, right. Not one of us, instructor or administrator, was prepared to deal with the consequences of such neo-draconian policy.

One instructor quit halfway through the program, basing their decision on the new hell of the past couple of summers and lack of program response to-date. This was bad, and what followed was worse: they gave me her dozen or so students, to add to my dozen students in our Critical Thinking seminar. So this morphed from a dignified college-level seminar to a full-blown high school class of about twenty-five. Then, worse went to worst: the only room they had available for our doubled group was, so they insisted, a computer classroom. And if worst can get even worse—and violating grammatical law, believe me, it can—the computers were along the walls, with no ability to move seating to get students away from them. AND if even worse than worst can get apocalyptic—there was no way to disable the internet.

You know what came next: twenty-five adolescents, in agonizing screen withdrawal, found themselves back on the sweet e-teat of mindless distraction. To bloody hell with any lesson plan I might have brought, however HS-student-friendly I might have hoped this would be. Honestly, I can only call the experience phenomenal as I had never dealt with the total inability to get my students' attention, much less get them on task with my intended class activities. In fact, one lad, previously known to me as a sweet kid, swiveled his head with its glazed eyes to me when I stood behind him, begging to know "what is so interesting that you all won't even look at me?" and hissed, "Why don't you fuck off." I had never in my twenty years of teaching to that date been spoken to this way, by a student.

But honestly, how can an English instructor, with her "critical thinking" nonsense, compete with what they had quickly plugged into online: images of nubile bodies, barely or unclothed, some even foregrounding their private parts? One simply cannot imagine the challenge of trying to teach logical fallacies in the presence of illogical phalluses. For once in my career, I felt I had a problem I couldn't handle.

Having an unmanageable problem should be a thrilling call to action for any true educator, right? Not to mention that I had eight more class meetings scheduled with this group. I had to do something and make it work.

So, the next afternoon, I showed up with three dozen doughnuts and a killer lesson plan. They could go onto their preferred sites, no problem, as long as they answered four "critical thinking" questions for me:

1. What is this site? (Knowledge)
2. What does it consist of? (Analysis)
3. Why is it so compelling that you will not be moved from it? (Evaluation)
4. How does this information contribute to your successful future? (Application)

This was my first active effort to bridge the divide and enter the new world. The doughnuts distracted them from their screens while I explained the day's drill. Lo and behold, they accepted my page of questions into their sugar-glazed fingers, nodded assent, and turned to the task! I watched them pull up their content, study it closely, and then write their responses. I was beyond relieved and felt I had stumbled, however awkwardly and hesitantly, into the pedagogical future: students thinking critically about mindless media! Assuming that this could even happen, I couldn't wait for us to regroup and share our answers.

My desperate hopes ended when our program administrator—a forlorn creature who, herself, I now realize, had long lost hope in anything but pure rule-driven force—popped into my classroom and saw what was holding the interest of my class, on screens no less, in spite of the strict program rule forbidding contact with screens of any kind. You can imagine what happened next. Unable to defend our pedagogically legitimate lesson underway, I was ejected from the classroom and then, after seventeen years of faithful service, fired for "allowing" our students to surf porn during class.

To this day, I cannot disagree with their decision. Surely a stronger-minded instructor could have redirected the students' attention. If such an instructor exists, I trust they will receive the Nobel Prize in Teaching, which should be invented for just this occasion. Throw in a Peace prize, too.

But show me twenty-five phone-deprived, super-hormonal teenagers with the renewed ability to access a world of porn, and I'll show you an undistractable crowd, excepting a minute's sugar snack, that is. I myself cannot assure you that I would not have done the same at that age.

That the program did not give me the chance to explain or defend myself, I believe was wrong. Not that they would have understood, as "rules are rules"; but I could have explained to them the problem and retroactively, the solution: get us out of the computer classroom. I had begged for this the first week, but it was futile under the auspices of institutional room-scheduling forces. I had to content myself with my knowledge that the punishment was built into the crime, in these ways:

- They had a couple weeks left and had to find another instructor for these monsters, and
- They'd have to deal with trying to keep their campers off phones and screens for the rest of the program, summer after summer, with the problem exponentially worsening, which I would not.

I got paid the rest of my program salary anyway, because I went to the university provost to demand why institution computers were not disabled for pornography. For this, they had no answer because there was none. I claimed that I was "traumatized" by the images the students had pulled up and by the fact that my repeated early requests for another regular classroom had been ignored and denied. I claimed that this situation had damaged the tender minds of our most vulnerable students. Amazing how powerful that "traumatized" charge is, not to mention "most vulnerable students." Don't mess with an English teacher; that was the admin's own institutional learning outcome.

We in education know that for everything we try in the classroom, outcome successful or unsuccessful, we must file a "Learning Outcome." As you can see from the above, my efforts proved unsuccessful with regards to the students. However, there arose from this a solid LO for the instructor: never try to pit "critical thinking," in all of its academic and professional glory and demand, against dick pics. This is an unwinnable battle, so don't even try. Accept your failure, even your dismissal, and move on.

The Case of the Cellular Colluders

When suffering severe burnout, direct a Special Program for Advanced Students!

After all, in so doing, you'll get to hang out with the best and brightest; and you won't have to deal with some of the challenges, often daunting, of teaching in Gen Pop. When I got permission to teach this special curriculum, I thought my ship had finally come in. The hitch in my hope, the error in my enthusiasm over this proved to be my failure to remember one of life's most solid truths: you only ever trade one set of problems for another.

A problem arose from our need to attract students into the program. "Too much work!" "I'm not that smart!" "I'd have to read stuff!" When we were able to feed a bit of scholarship money into the offer, interest grew, and I managed to lure a couple dozen into the deal.

For the most part, the program worked out well; I still keep up with some of these, who reached for the higher bar and made good of it. We eventually lured a couple other colleagues into teaching our classes. We attended conferences. We won awards. For the most part, all who participated profited from and enjoyed the experience of pitching high and earning the Special Scholar distinction.

But recall that we were a bit desperate for bodies, if not minds. Some of our students were less than worthy. I do not refer to the one who, predicting the tl;dr text lingo, regularly returned explanations of "too long, didn't read" for why they could or would not write a one-page summary of a four-page article. Nor do I mean the one who claimed they "didn't learn a THING in my class" because everything—the greatest essays across the most compelling themes of the past millennium—was "BORING." I do not refer to the one who got expelled for bullying a classmate; apparently, this continued a long tradition from their high school experience. I would not be surprised to learn that it has persisted to this day.

I want to share the tale of Fricka and Fracka, who nearly brought my career down with their plotting. However, I do not blame them, as they fell victim to the diabolical instrument of their treachery. If my colleagues, called in to help adjudicate the case, had not been wimps or at least ignorant, as I was, of the true nature of the crime, F&F might indeed have lost their paradise, which was to be viewed by everyone who knew them as perfect and incapable of wrongdoing—as I learned in several painful, vociferous meetings.

I call them Fricka and Fracka to celebrate their Viking invincibility. What did they do to evoke such Wagnerian drama in our little program? They cheated on their final; it's called "collusion," one of the seven deadly sins of academic dishonesty. But how, you might ask, did they accomplish this since they were sitting across from each other in the testing room?

My naïve claim, based on missing seven out of twenty-five multiple-choice questions (more than 25%), could have been challenged as random, yes. But the identical answers, some of them obviously odd and wrong? Still… Let's move on to the short-answer questions, of which they were to choose three out of eight. Yes, reader, F&F chose the same three, and their short answers were nearly identical. Memory's kind handmaiden often causes us to forget the more absurd unpleasantries of our everyday existence; however,

I will attempt to recall one of these answers: "Ralf [sic] Waldo Emerson's important modernistic philosophy significantly influenced the Surealist [sic] painters in their grasp of mankind's eternal detachment." Gotcha, ladies. Yet, they had indeed been sitting across the room from each other during the test. Physics aside, habeas corpus: I had the test answers, indisputable evidence of collusion!

But no... the tribunal that followed—a perfect storm of howling protest, hurt feelings, parental threats, collegial hedging, and administrative cowering—could not begin to address, much less rectify, the wrong. The worst was my colleagues, called upon to review the case and provide backup, in their feedback: "Did you see them looking at each other's papers?" Of course, the answer was no, I didn't. But surely the evidence is enough... It wasn't. This taught me my policy ever since: without "ocular proof," there can be no crime. That ocular proof must be in the form of a photograph, the original essay, or other direct empirical evidence of cheating. Even then, enough belligerent indignation is often enough to weary the accuser into giving up. So, I had to drop the charge and award these two the mediocre test grades they earned, being careful not to let this endanger their final averages, lest a lower number be living proof of the damage inflicted by their paranoid instructor's oppression of these little martyr saints.

However, this is not the tale's end. The last term day I had a visitor to my office, another member of that class. This young lady had indeed been bullied by F&F during high school, and she had been waiting for just this opportunity. "They had cell phones during the test."

Now, I know that it's hard to fathom the instructor's ignorance of this possibility but remember that this happened a good while ago, before she herself gave in and acquired the instrument of doom. But what did the informer mean? They didn't call each other to chat during the test!

"They messaged each other their answers." Just wow. "I watched them doing it." Apparently they even saw her watching them and didn't stop, so confident were they in the success of their history of terrorizing her into inaction. I had to explain to the informer that at this time, I could do nothing about it. "But, be comforted with this: they were stupid enough to message each other bad, wrong answers, which got them caught." We would both have to make do with our knowledge of that shame. I figured they would do it one day in Nursing School, where the crime would finally receive its due justice.

There are a couple of important lessons here. First, if you're going to cheat, at least cheat off someone who has the right answers. I enjoy explaining this to my students, who appreciate this obvious but, in a panic, often forgotten advice. Second, as I mentioned, I learned never to approach a cheater without hard and irrefutable proof, however exhausting and time-consuming the gathering of such evidence can be. If you can't just turn a blind eye and let a much more punitive context catch the perpetrators, saving you the soul-draining pursuit—just make sure that you're absolutely certain and can prove it.

Eventually, I learned that two can play the cyber-game when it comes to cheating. I had two freshman English pupils who kept submitting letter-perfect writing despite their second-language status and stage of education (just post-high school), where one might expect at least some lesser degree of language competency and idea sophistication. Yet, I never could pull up anything incriminating, on either TurnItIn, where the mere 0% match was a red flag, or Google searches, even advanced ones. Finally, one day during an in-class writing, I decided to activate the little "owl-eyes" icon on my instructor's computer up front. What might this do? It brought up the screens of all my students, allowing me to watch them in progress. And lo and behold, these two were pulling up essays on our assigned topic in their own language and having them Google-translated. I took screenshots of every step of that process for both. Imagine their surprise when, turned in to the office for plagiarism and after hurling every level of charge at me for my paranoia and "ethnic prejudice," our chairman produced those screenshots.

The surveillance state, however treacherous, does have its forensic uses.

CHAPTER 6: LEARNING, KIDNAPPED

Academic Dishonesty, Prof. Alexa, and the "End of College"

> In an abundance of water, the fool is thirsty.
>
> —Bob Marley, "Rat Race"

> They have beaten us.
>
> —A Colleague, 21st Century Academic Forum, Harvard University, 2014

I had already a complete draft of this chapter when AI Chatbot GPT was released. So, it might be the case that you can stop reading now, as none of the following matters since any resemblance to the world I once knew—where plagiarism was at first laborious, then easier, then routine, but if not preventable, still detectable and prosecutable—might be lost to the cyber-wind. Thus, these prefatory remarks are necessary and significant, marking the opening of a divide, dare I say an abyss which even the most intrepid wanderer would hesitate to bridge, out of exhaustion, anger, and finally, hopelessness.

If you've been off the grid, or care nothing about education, you might have avoided learning what ChatGPT is. Since you're reading this, ignorance of this nuclear attack is unlikely but in that case do Google it now. Basically, it's having a super-erudite and master researcher Alexa at your bidding: when you receive a writing (or math, or any other) assignment, just ask Professor Alexa, and she'll retrieve the information and write the paper for you. Moreover, as a philosophy professor at Furman University (interviewed on CNN, 12/25/22) observes, this service is instantaneous, free, and pretty much undetectable. If you listen closely, you might hear the collective moan from every educator out here.

Does ChatGPT, which will also exponentially increase in capability and undetectability (due, no doubt to the market—can't imagine specifically how this will happen, but with every student on earth using it, there has to be a way to profit handsomely from it), signal a new sub-paradigm shift: a call that we must completely change our whole evaluation system? And thus likewise our way of studying and learning? Hear the collective groan from faculty whose patience and faith have already been tested so sorely.

A bit of history, personal and scholarly

To my students' delight, I confess to them my own experience with college cheating. Note the singular noun: to the best of my recollection, I did it only once, and understandably, on an astrophysics final. The course was supposed to be Astronomy, where I had planned to learn about the surface conditions of Venus from the octogenarian professor beloved by all for his cute German accent, quirkiness, and providing A's, irrespective of actual effort, to all who enrolled. Sadly, he had died suddenly over the holiday break, and I found myself in the erratic orbit of his replacement, a young astrophysicist from Cal Tech. I was in trouble. I had to pass this one lab science requirement to graduate, and learning the material was not an option. At the close of the first class session, Dr. Poindexter had filled an entire blackboard with one equation and was starting on a second when the proverbial bell rang, sending me reeling from the room in hopeless terror.

Subsequently I made some friends in the class, crackerjack physics nerds, and they promised to coach me before the final. So far I was carrying a D, if that. Half of the course grade depended on this final so without help, I was lost. However, on the day before the exam, I followed a trail of marijuana smoke across campus and ended up at their dorm room, about the same time they cracked open their firsts from a case of beer. "No worries—just sit between us tomorrow," they reassured. At this point, what other choice did I have?

The next day, with the help of my stoner geeks, I did take and pass the exam well enough to squeeze a passing C- in the course. But in a vicious twist, karma, that unavoidable bitch, got me good. I won't put the details here in print but trust me. And my story of cheating and karma always seemed to make an impression on my students, certainly more so than any number and intensity of warnings, threats, syllabus anti-AD blurbs, beggings, pleadings, bustings and any other kind of attempted deterrent.

Students have always cheated. I am sure that there is some mention of this in Socrates; one of the reasons he warned against teaching students the alphabet must have included the point that if you write it down, somebody can copy it and use it for their own gain. When I was in college back in the Stone(d) Age, a dorm-mate got busted for plagiarism in a shocking incident. Postponing writing her essay until the last minute, of course, she had plumbed the depths of our campus graduate library, a no-undergrad's land if ever there was one, and excavated an ancient, moldy tome from which she copied part of a chapter to submit as her essay. Imagine her shock when, a week later, her grizzled professor called her in and produced the very same tome from his desk drawer. It turned out he had been one of its editors, a fact that had escaped her in her joyful relief over finding this book on her topic, buried deep in the grad lib sub-basement, surely lost forever to all but her own eyes. Murphy's Law, karma's milder cousin, also lies ever in wait for the desperate.

Students used to have to sit next to the prepared "smart" ones and copy from their test papers, risking being caught by the instructor, whose word back then would've been enough for a solid bust. I once had a couple of burly jock types following a nerdy classmate around the room, quiz to quiz, and wondered how these could be buddies. Shortly before the final, the nerdy one came to my office and told me that these behemoths had threatened him: let us copy all your papers, or we'll make it rough for you. He was scared to the point of being ill. I was furious but I had a good plan. "Come and take your final in my office the day before," I told him, "but then come to the classroom and fake-take it that day, making sure to put in mostly wrong answers." My final test, a term review, counted 25% of their final course grade. On test day, I watched the perps flagrantly copy their classmate's test paper; they even saw me watching them and probably wondered why I was doing nothing to stop them.

The two knowledge thieves miserably failed the final, each with a score of about 12 or so. This guaranteed them a no-pass in the course. (We had also had a couple of papers, and theirs had been mediocre C's at best; they'd had to plagiarize before the internet, which had evidently required too much effort.) How I enjoyed receiving them in my office where, wild-eyed, they insisted that "something was wrong with my test"—you could feel the steam coming off when they compared their papers to the answer key. "But there's NO WAY I could have gotten all these wrong." Really? How so "no way"?

I have so, so many, but I must share another notable case or two. There were the two ladies who submitted the exact same essay, raising the red flag, and I easily pulled up the original essay. I printed it off and put it right between their two copies. When I called them into my office, they indignantly denied the crime. Even when I showed them the three copies, they continued to plead innocence, accusing me of all kinds of error and malice. I finally shut them down when I told them I would submit their names to the local university's Parapsychology Institute, as surely they were the strongest cases of ESP on record. Another student, submitting an essay straight from the internet, explained thus: "Oh, I didn't mean to submit that one as my paper. I just happened to see this one on a computer screen in the library; I read it and thought, 'Oh, wouldn't Dr. Sapp love this one!' So I printed and submitted that paper by accident, instead of my own." "Oh, and I guess you accidentally put your own name and our course information in the top left of page one." You just have to try to be smarter if you're dishonest.

Cheating was not invented by the internet, of course, but the latter has made the former much easier and, of late, more undetectable and unprosecutable.

Losing My Religion

The years went on, the cheating kept increasing, and I found myself expending way too much of my remaining precious life energy chasing perps and trying to gather enough evidence to dare to accuse them, much less prosecute and penalize. Becoming increasingly exhausted, I started to wonder if any of this was worth it anymore. I mean, I was spending an average of 15-20 minutes or more grading some ghost writer out there on the internet who would never even see my constructive feedback. My student who passed this fraud to me and about whom I presumably did care didn't learn anything. What about me? What did I gain? Then I had the epiphany: I didn't have to gain anything; I just didn't lose anything. I had made a good effort to do my job, and my pay didn't go down one nickel because the effort was on a bogus submission.

So I went to class and addressed my students: "I am worn out chasing cheaters. I refuse to do it anymore. My pay doesn't go down one nickel if you cheat. You don't learn anything, and somewhere down the line, that will trip you up big time. But that won't be my problem; I did my best to help you, but you rejected that help. So, cheaters out there, good luck when you're shoved into that booth and required to write, without internet or even a dictionary, that essay that will make or break your application." Silently, they stared at me during this speech. Then, we got down to business and had our class.

Lo and behold—I believe this helped when no other approach had. It seemed that I received more evidently honest efforts than ever before. Then, I was stressed because I had to spend so much time evaluating seriously flawed writing. Bless my students' hearts; some of them just couldn't win.

My epiphanic shift did relieve my stress while freeing up time and energy. I'd spend the 15-20 minutes evaluating each paper without having to tack on the extra time trying to find ocular proof of a presumed crime. My abdication was either a radical solution or a symptom of quiet quitting.

Of course, I always wondered how my colleagues dealt with all this. Either they didn't care, much less suffer, as much as I had, or they just resorted to the standard responses: "Oh, my students don't really cheat." Isn't it pretty to think so? "I make them hand-write everything in class." How nineteenth-century of you. Plus, reading all that handwriting? Oy! "Don't you use Turn-It-In?" I do, but it often doesn't work. Hussin & Ismail, in their 2013 "Plagiarism: More than Meets the Eye," call plagiarism a "taboo" topic among educators: no one wants to acknowledge, much less talk about such a hopeless topic. As Pecorari & Petric point out, "plagiarism has been described as a sin, vice, disease, cancer, plague, stealing and a crime." As we did not train in law enforcement or medicine, we do not feel equipped to respond to the dangers and miseries inherent in treating plagiarism. Finally, exhausted graders just don't have the will to deal with plagiarism in a system that is so rigged against their efforts to stop or even ameliorate the problem.

I have repeatedly referenced the dire necessity of producing hard evidence of plagiarism. Even this usually doesn't stop the accused from virulent attacks on the judgment, accuracy, credibility, inclusiveness and even eyesight of the accuser. However, with such proof, charges can be officially made resulting in various degrees of wrist-slapping by institutions terrified of lawsuits or lowered enrollments. "Performance-based funding" threatens institutions that dare to keep students from graduating, for any reason, however valid. Instructors have a legitimate fear of putting themselves through the ordeal of making a charge that could turn on them; after all, isn't it their fault that they couldn't stop this student from cheating? Didn't they teach her well enough to be able to do the work herself? I'm not claiming that such turnabout is the norm; however, its mere possibility is enough to dampen the fervor of an instructor who doesn't really feel like playing morality police in the first place.

How else is the "system rigged against the efforts" of those who would try to stop plagiarism? I have mentioned such as the Turn-It-In plagiarism checker available to learning platforms and individual instructors. How excited were we to learn that the very tool that enabled massive and easy plagiarism, the internet, could be used, at the stroke of a key, to bust that plagiarism? Turn-It-In checks the submissions for matches in all the databases available to it, which is quite a few. Moreover, it produces a beautiful spreadsheet of those matches with percentage matched, along with other relevant information. How thrilling to screenshot an 80% match and attach it to the perp's zeroed submission? It looks very technical, data-driven— who could argue?

Recall Satan's promise that whatever good God would bring to his favorite creature, Satan would pervert. So it has gone with Turn-It-In. I started to see something curious occurring more and more often in the TII reports: a match of 0%. That is, zero percent of the language in the submission matched any other document out there. The fact that this would occur in a submission full of references and connections to other texts could only compound one's suspicions. But a zero-percent match slammed the door shut; the data have spoken! This writing is 100% original, then, to the point that it might have been written in Martian, which surely would have no match with any Earthly language strings.

I have not heavily researched this 0% match problem with TII, but even if I had, I likely would not have found helpful pronouncements. Studies exist, but I will rely here on my own experience. Teaching international students, I have recently seen letter-perfect papers from students who almost needed a translator to discuss matters with me in English. Yet, their submissions could be published unedited in the *College English* journal. This presents too much of a gap between oral and written literacy. I have assumed that Google Translate has become more sensitive to the nuances of English because in the past, bizarre diction and syntax called attention to this plagiarism method even when we could not prove it. However, we could call out the submission based on incomprehensible language; if I can't read it, it doesn't fly, and this is only reasonable.

However, nowadays I see students downloading papers from their own language and having them Google-translated, and they look pretty good. My international students grab their phones for help with just about everything we do in our ESL classes: reading, writing, listening, speaking, grammar; and they do it right in front of me as if this were just the right way to master a second language. Have the internet do it for you, and why not? TII does not have the translation-detection capacity, to the best of my knowledge. The other day I returned a 0%-match paper to a student, saying "This looks OK overall, but do notice that you must use capital letters for proper nouns and end punctuation"—there was none of either in her submission. "Oh, that's a translation from the internet," she explained, without a hint of guilt or shame. "And a bad one," was my only reply.

Educators have written about the unreliability or just weakness of TII as reliable ocular proof. In an especially indignant piece, John Warner warns us of a feature that TII purported to add, where in the wake of the essay-mill plague (see discussion below), it would include the capability to compare the submission's writing to previous submissions by the same student and check for "considerable divergence from previous work." Warner sees this as violation on several dystopian levels. In the end, he declares himself free of the need for such burdensome and suspicious ordeals, as he "hasn't had a plagiarism case in a decade." He has achieved this nirvana by giving them topics based on their personal experience, making assignments process-based, and making them "show evidence of the journey on the way to the destination" (*Inside Higher Ed*). I hate to break this to Prof. Warner, but I have had students plagiarize every step of a process; did he imagine this is impossible? I have had students plagiarize their own personal narratives. They probably have plagiarized text messages to me. Trust me that for many, if they can find it on Google and now have Chat write it, they don't feel the need to produce it themselves.

In fact, investigators have found that our principal partner in crime, the internet, has innocently encouraged if not plagiarism outright, application errors in our ability to evaluate work. Students make mistakes while searching for information online, mis-cite sources, and some believe that if it's on the internet, it's general knowledge and doesn't need to be cited. Since my capital-letter-deprived plagiarist was assigned to write about her hometown, she didn't see any reason to make it original; after all, anyone can Google that information, which is just a collection of tourist-attractive facts. Effective internet research requires a new skill set, one we assume our digital natives have, but it turns out that a great many do not have as this results from careful training. Benignly put, "Lack of such skills leads to source-use problems, including internet plagiarism. As Stapleton concludes, 'new tools and resources come with caveats'" (Pecorari and Petric 298). All of my colleagues who are still hanging on to shreds of hope, as well as nerve, attempting to teach even the simplified MLA citation style, are feeling my pain here.

Now we turn to the most pernicious, destructive and disheartening front of war against plagiarism, before the apocalyptic ChatGPT, that is: "contract cheating." Once this came on the scene, we were lost and wandering about, flailing for ways to counter this crime that threatened to topple my faith in the whole enterprise of higher education. The only good news is that ChatGPT, being for now free, is contract-cheating's own apocalypse. Live by the sword, die by the sword.

"In 2014, Owings and Nelson reviewed what they called 'The Essay Industry' and estimated that it 'has annual revenues somewhere upward of $100 million with estimated minimum profits of $50 million'" (Awdry & Newton). Compelling stories there are of English teachers who, having abandoned all hope, quit their day jobs and hired on writing for these companies, doubling their annual income. These "essay mills" are variously illegal around the world; most all advertise themselves under seductive marketing and promises of being "100 plagiarism-free." A quick Google glance reveals the euphemistic, "Essay Ace is a top-ranked service available to support all of your college writing needs"; the sympathetic, "Essay help allows you not to worry about deadlines and devote your time to whatever desired" [seriously!]; the straightforward, "Have a native essay writer do your task from scratch for a student-friendly price of $10 per page"; and even the elitist, "Harvard-educated essay specialist will help you get into the Ivy League" by writing your application essays for you. My students and I classified these as part of a marketing-rhetoric lesson; they fondly recall my purple face as I screamed, "How dare they claim to be 'plagiarism-free'? They ARE PLAGIARISM ITSELF!"

"The use of paid third parties by students does appear to be increasing," reported Awdry and Newton in 2019. Why wouldn't it? My own students have confessed to me rampant usage of these sites. "You haven't graded a single essay written by me," one insisted. One argued, guilelessly, "Why would I spend the time writing when I can get this?" I admit I didn't have an answer better than, "Well, you won't have learned anything," to which he nodded acknowledgement, at least. A 2018 report broke down "the contract cheating problem into five segments: bespoke essay sites, using friends and family, discussion sites, tutorial sites and auction sites." Other investigators classify these sordid operations a bit differently: "academic custom writing, online labour [sic] markets, pre-written essay banks, file-sharing sites and paid exam takers" (Ellis et al).

Add increasingly sophisticated Google Translate capabilities, and all of this can be had in just about any world language, to be translated and submitted in my for-credit ESL writing courses. My students tell me that in their native countries, there exist great "factories" producing assignments, and those lucky enough to work there are paid double or triple what they can earn in a normal job available to them. I once had a student of limited ability, as exhibited in our in-class writings, submit a syntactically perfect four-page essay, with a Works Cited page containing five outside scholarly sources and correct in-text citations throughout. (This was my biggest clue that the paper wasn't honest; I have come to believe that it just might be impossible to teach effective in-text citation anymore, much less do it myself.) Did I mention that this masterpiece was accomplished in a 90-minute, in-class writing activity? Yes, I let them use their devices to type and upload their efforts on our learning platform's Assignments site. I'm not reading ninety minutes' worth of scribblings on paper from twenty-five students, no ma'am. My chair, who shares my belief in sparing our students distress whenever possible, asked me how I could be sure the paper was plagiarized." Sure," I responded, "the student found five scholarly articles, read them, developed her argument, incorporated the source information, developed four pages of complex discussion, effectively cited, and checked the whole to correct any and all syntax issues—all in ninety minutes." "But can you prove it?" Now this, unfortunately, was a legitimate question. It passed TurnItIn with a zero percent match, and all my life-consuming efforts running strings through Google Advanced Search yielded nothing.

"Oh yeah," a colleague replied upon hearing of this miraculous accomplishment. "The student ordered it 'rush' from one of those essay mills; for an extra hefty fee, they can return the product within just about whatever time you need." And did I mention that this in-class writing activity was a practice one, just to prepare for an upcoming in-class essay test, and received only a modicum of daily-grade credit? The student knew this, but the compulsion and ease of acquisition made the transaction irresistible. "Win whoso may, all is for sale," quipped Chaucer's Wife of Bath a millennium ago. If you'd rather waste your money than use a learning opportunity, who am I to protest? That's your business, after all! No, it's not, it IS my business. It's a waste of my precious remaining earthly moments trying to solve the mystery of your perfidy, and more importantly, it's a waste of your classmates' time—the honest ones, that is—who could benefit from my application of those moments to their own efforts.

Why do so many commit this flagrant and costly act of cheating? Echoing my student, my quick answer is, because they can. The internet has made it so easy, it's almost ridiculous not to cheat (especially when doing so frees you to do "whatever desired"), whereas back in my time, cheating required digging through musty library stacks and then laboriously hand-copying the borrowed information. Now, with minimal literacy skills and at the touch of a key, you can borrow the performance of a Pulitzer-worthy writer. One of the biggest tells about the ChatGPT takeover is the almost total absence of any grammatical error in their submissions even as the perps compose barely-readable emails and the occasional in-class submission. And I'm not likely to call you out on anything either, at least not in the absence of ocular proof of the crime. As I have mentioned before, trying to bust cheating pulls the weary instructor into a cluster of trouble: evasions, accusations, interrogations, threats, and all forms of soul-sickening abdication of administrative support. These essay mills and contract cheating opportunities appeared at the time as the coup de grâce, freeing instructors from any hope of success and thus any need to make the effort.

As Pauli Alin accurately perceives, "such confrontation presents a difficult problem, which may explain why instructors may choose to do nothing even when they suspect that a cheating company has been used. Part of the problem is that the instructors are actually faced with a two-stage problem: firstly, how to reliably justify the suspicion that cheating by a cheating company may have occurred, and secondly, how to make a document-based case that this is so" (6). Alin proposes the ultimate goal of successful proof and action: "Ideally, such prosecution would require minimal use of the instructor's time and energy, as well as stop the student's use of the cheating companies in the future" (5). Ideally, indeed. Like the gun issue in the face of our national violence epidemic—how to take the guns out of their hands to prevent the handful of psycho killers from doing their worst—how can this ever-proliferating profit-glutton industry be stopped?

Awdry and Newton conclude, vaguely, that "It will continue to be imperative that the issue of commercial contract cheating is explored from a variety of angles to allow as full a picture as possible to be painted by the staff, students, institutions, companies, and writers. Without this, any sector or local responses are likely to be ineffective." Pretty language, with its it-cleft hedge, its gentle metaphor, and its confident agent list. But you can put lipstick on a pig, and it's still a pig. Add to the obstacles intrinsic to the problem a reasonable list of extrinsic ones: overwhelmed (and underpaid, under-supported) instructors, poor administrative backup, exhausting battles with offended accusees and their parents, and more. Thomas Lancaster opines that "The industry flourishes when the education system operates within a free-market model where students are sorted out according to grades, and knowledge and education are considered commodities" (2). In my own wanderings over the decades, I have perceived, and cannot deny, ever-increasing tendencies along these lines. Too many of my colleagues will be too familiar with the confrontation, "But I paid for this grade," now formalized into the requirement that the credit paid for pay off in the student's future desirability for being hired and thus their livelihood and life.

If this weren't bad enough, there is the normalizing of cheating in institutions that are calling it something else: "culturally relative models," neoliberal "shifts in concepts of ownership," along with attacks on Western "private ownership models," and more shades of pig lipstick to cover the bare fact that way too many of our students cheat their way through their education. As I have always asked my students, "Do you want your surgeon to have cheated their way through school? How do you feel about driving over a bridge designed by a cheating engineering student?" They enjoy my paranoia and, I believe, find a jot of truth in it; however, *ars longa, vita brevis*—and there's a lot of desired whatever out there, easy and even now free, for the taking.

CHAPTER 7: TEA WITH A DEMON (BOT) IN STOCKHOLM (SYNDROME)

> All technology has the property of the Midas touch; whenever a society develops an extension of itself, all other functions of that society tend to be transmuted to accommodate that new form; once any new technology penetrates a society, it saturates every institution of that society. —Marshall McLuhan

> [A]cademics have a duty to enter into the public sphere unafraid to take positions and generate controversy, functioning as moral witnesses, raising political awareness, and making connections to those elements of power and politics often hidden from public view.
>
> —Henry Giroux

In her blogpost, "Why You Should Invite Your Inner Demons to Tea," Elaine Smookler explains: "When it feels like a storm is brewing inside you—a potent mix of anxiety, jealousy, anger, and other difficult emotions—you might be inclined to turn away. But that rarely makes them dissipate, so you might as well invite them in and get to know them better." This chapter is about an educator's attempt to, if not come to terms with, get to know one particular external demon: one that descended upon us in the past year, ravenously gobbling up our students' creativity, integrity and autonomy and threatening to destroy any last chance we might have for a legitimate English course. Just when we thought that plagiarism couldn't get any worse, it did, to bring in another apt metaphor of violence, in the ChatGPT carpet-bombing of education. I knew from the start that *they had beaten us.* How and where to go, from here?

Answering this has been my task for the past months. In previous chapters, I have mentioned conversations about the demon bot and some colleagues' efforts to assuage my fear and anger by offering their newfound enthusiasm for such a handy tool and support in their classes. However, I had continued adamantly to resist even trying to learn about the bot, along with the notion that doing so would bring any benefit to my students or me. I knew, though, that this attitude would have to change, even in the face of doubt that it could. Educators have this great habit of making themselves see even the worst of situations as a "learning opportunity," so I proceeded in that direction and was immediately gifted, in August 2023, with a conference opportunity: "AI and Education." (I am not giving the actual title or further identification information not because I plan to say anything terrible about this event but rather out of respect for the fine three-day effort they did make. Of course, I had my red pen scribbling continuously throughout; I had/have a bad attitude that colors every effort I make to make peace with the demon.)

I will instead summarize this conference with the words of Adam Kirsch, who in his 2014 *New Republic* article "Technology Is Taking Over English Departments: The false promise of the digital humanities," pointed to the core motivation of both the bot itself and its proponents:

> The language here is the language of scholarship, but the spirit is the spirit of salesmanship—the very same kind of hyperbolic, hard-sell approach we are so accustomed to hearing about the Internet, or about Apple's latest utterly revolutionary product. Fundamental to this kind of persuasion is the undertone of menace, the threat of historical illegitimacy and obsolescence. Here is the future, we are made to understand: we can either get on board or stand athwart it and get run over.

All throughout the conference, while receiving a lot of encouragement about how to bring AI responsibly and ethically (the two key words of the AI challenge) into our teaching, we were reminded that failing to do so "puts your students' futures at risk." To make the failure of or resistance to technology-tool advancement a moral or ethical issue seems to me a grievous confusion about the mission of education. However, in an economy that has shifted the focus and goal of learning from the message to the medium, where McLuhan's prophecy is fully realized, this conference's dire warning makes sense. If we don't teach our students how the tools of education direct and inform not only their learning but also its future application, we might as well just admit that we want to ruin their lives. Never mind that getting access to these tools threatens, for many, to widen the Digital Divide in its original meaning: the gap between the "haves" with easy and guaranteed continued access to the medium and the "have-nots" who, due to their geographic or cultural location or to a lack of desire and will to engage with the relentless bombardment of innovations, cannot or will not use the medium.

Combine this "medium as message" with the idea expressed in previous chapters that reading and writing are undergoing a radical identity shift and that writing, especially, is now a matter of digital manipulation and experimentation rather than comprehension of a given text. Kirsch continues, in 2014, to offer what might now be considered an archaic and irrelevant judgment:

> The best thing that the humanities could do at this moment, then, is not to embrace the momentum of the digital, the tech tsunami, but to resist it and to critique it. This is not Luddism; it is intellectual responsibility. Is it actually true that reading online is an adequate substitute for reading on paper? If not, perhaps we should not be concentrating on digitizing our books but on preserving and circulating them more effectively. Are images able to do the work of complex discourse? If not, and reasoning is irreducibly linguistic, then it would be a grave mistake to move writing away from the center of a humanities education.

Recently, one of my students, when confronted with my belief (read: knowledge) that his paper submission was entirely a product of a moment's click on the ChatGPT site, offered this: "I don't get it; you asked for a paper on this topic, and here's a paper on this topic." The paper did indeed check off all the rubric items and admirably at that; one might say that it delved deeply into the potential for nuanced community engagement of the topic ("delved," "ubiquitous," "nuanced," and "community engagement" being some of the bot's favorite academic diction displays). Struggling to suppress the shudder of horror running through my very core, I found myself at a loss to explain it to him any other way than recourse to not only a dying notion but also an illogical one in a consumer-commodity culture. What would it mean to explain to him that what I wanted was not a "paper" as a product but his thinking as a process: how he put his mind to the various steps of the assignment and learned and grew from exercising his own faculties? In an ever-increasingly "collaborative," "hive-mind" conception of literacy, how important is individual thought and effort? Never mind that without these, there cannot be any legitimate mind in the collaboration or hive: humans are not bees. And what has happened to creativity and autonomy? But after all, we don't conjure and create the products we consume; we go online, click a key, and order them from Amazon.

In his groundbreaking 2010 work, *The Shallows: What the Internet Is Doing to Our Brains*, Nicholas Carr observes that the internet's commodity-driven platform (as the M.O. of its fundamental purpose of mining our data for mercenary gain) has, along with "[giving] us powerful new tools for finding information, expressing ourselves, and conversing with others" —its undeniable boons standing as the strong counterargument for all I've offered in this book—"also turns us into lab rats constantly pressing levers to get tiny pellets of social or intellectual nourishment" (117). Carr argues that the old model of reflection and delay necessarily involved in thinking and "weighing a decision" has been disrupted by the information pellet-dispensing medium that, in his view, is "a cacophony of stimuli [that] short-circuits both conscious and unconscious thought, preventing our minds from thinking either deeply or creatively" (119). In my digitally formed student's brain, by typing in the ChatGPT command and hitting "send" to receive the whole paper within seconds, he was simply hitting the dispenser and getting the desired pellet.

Recall Adam Gopnik's "Ever-Wasers," those who consider every new tech invasion the same as it ever was: as it was when the printing press came along, or the internet itself, or social media rising to dominance as means of communication, so it is now with generative AI and such as ChatGPT. The Ever-Waser will recommend that we think about Chat the same way, perhaps referring to Nicholas Carr's brilliant chapter "The Deepening Page," where he gives a meticulous history of the evolution of reading according to the medium, from cave people scratching on stones to digital people scratching comments in social media. It's all writing, isn't it? No less than linguist John McWhorter has a wonderful (yes, it can happen) TED Talk on texting as a new legitimate mode of writing that he cutely and aptly calls "fingered speech." As an English instructor, I welcome all new media and modes of writing as this is ever our task: to stay on top of (d)evolutions in literacy, seeing how our students are writing and discerning how we might, using our tools and tricks from the past, help them do it more effectively for that medium and at the same time add to our own tool belt of the trade.

But what can we do when our students are not writing and are just pushing the pellet dispenser to release a machine-written product? How do we adapt to and serve that? Who or what can we serve under the new overlord? Do we just train technology to analyze and evaluate these pellets in a system where, to quote James Bridle in his ominously titled *New Dark Age: Technology and the End of the Future*, "The act of writing, of generating information, becomes part of a mesh of data and data generation, read as well as written by machines" (124). Again, no human seems to be learning anything but how to push the right buttons; however, the machine, the AI in the machine, is the learning winner as it ravenously absorbs all of the data to be crunched and mobilized in further advancement of the machines.

"You're being ridiculous," you might be thinking right now. "No one expects to have to grade obviously plagiarized assignments." We will teach our students how NOT to use it for "unethical" purposes! We will make this work! Through all of the conversations, articles, webinars and trainings I've had so far, the AI reception among colleagues seems to be predominantly one of curiosity, excitement and optimism. Sarah Newman, Harvard professor and leader of the AI Pedagogy Project observes that these are very exciting times to be educators. I have just ordered and received a handsome 350-page tome, apparently self-published by author Yvonne Ho in 2023, and entitled *Writing in the Age of AI: ChatGPT Unleashed by ChatGPT for Teachers and Students*. Putting aside for the moment that ominous "ChatGPT unleashed by ChatGPT," I see that it's a gorgeous book with twelve chapters covering just about every type of definition, exemplification, lesson plan and more for comprehensive use of the bot in the composition classroom. I haven't started going through it yet; I just let it lie in state on my desk and stare at it, the rat before the swaying snake. Will it change my mind and recruit me into the optimism team?

Would I want this to happen? Let us return to our tea party...

Tea and Tells

Over our tea, I can share with the demon that even though they are the Prince of Cyber-Lies, in a short time we instructors have become wise to their ways. I will share some of the main tells we have learned to see right away.

Dubious Diction

Now we will delve into the ubiquitous topic of what are arguably Chat's favorite words. A number of sites are now tallying Chat's favorite words; my favorites so far include these, to name a few: adhere, arguably, comprehensive, delve, dynamic, embark, excel, intricate, landscape, leverage, multifaceted, nuanced, pivotal, realm, tapestry, vibrant ("Emergent Tech"). I've even seen "a vibrant tapestry," although it might have been "nuanced" after all. I finally had to look up "leverage" due to seeing it so many times and not being sure how it was being used—an uncertainty certainly sharable with the putative authors, if they even made an effort to read the dispensed pellet-document themselves. There are plenty more of these terms along with phrases: "delving into the intricacies of," "navigating the complexities of," "it is important to consider," etc. By far, "delve" is the winner; delving students might as well call me on the phone to confess that they just generated their five-page paper in two minutes (maybe faster) with Chat.

Arid Affect

"Although these are terms that statistically appear more frequently in ChatGPT outputs than in regular human-authored text, the mere fact that a document contains some of them does not prove that it was created by ChatGPT," the site reminds us ("Emergent Tech"). I would say that it does prove it when an email from the same student is diction compromised: "hey coud you tell me what im supposd to do for the home work i dont get it" and in some cases, functionally illiterate or unreadable. Such ill-wrought messages do not come often, certainly; however, when this emailer finally embarks on an intricate and multifaceted, not to mention comprehensive yet nuanced tapestry of knowledge about this assignment, call me suspicious!

Once, when I dared challenge such a writer about this elevated diction, I received the response, "i used a thesaurus when i wrote my eassy" [sic]. A thesaurus? Did they also use a wayback machine? Not convinced!

I have compared reading Chat's output, shall I say "landscape," to wearily traversing a verbal desert, thirsty and eager for any sustaining sips of human foible. One will find no oasis of interestingly flawed human reason or, for Webster's sake, plain language. Chat's output is flat yet elevated, dry, numbingly predictable, and as dull as the worst textbook one has ever had to plow through in an all-nighter for a hated course. I never knew how much I enjoyed my students' lapses and need for my TurnItIn Quickmarks until now; when they would wax apologetic about their self-perceived substandard efforts, I'd reassure them: "If you came into my class knowing everything, I'd feel pretty useless here." Now, I long for a flawed effort with mistakes and misfires that call me into the action I was trained for. In fact, I miss terrible sentences, which leads me ("is pivotal") to our next tell.

Sanitized syntax

We instructors now realize that about a year ago, we stopped seeing any grammar or punctuation mistakes in student writing. While the internet warns that Chat's grammar isn't perfect, it has seemed pretty much so to me. A year ago, I was regularly Quickmarking away in TurnItIn for the inevitable Sentence Fragments, Comma Splices, Run-Ons, and more; occasionally, I'd have the pleasure of explaining Parallelism and Dangling Modifiers and writing "Let's eat Grandma" to show that commas save lives! Now, in any twenty submissions, no more than a half-dozen papers will have even one of these fun issues.

On the other hand, emails or any assignments calling for a more personal narrative style of writing will be fairly squirming with them. That is, if the writer hasn't used the bot for these as well. I have recently learned that Chat is getting really good at generating personal narratives: just feed in the prompt, a few of your life details, and boom, an eloquent little anecdote. Some use it to provide peer reviews and even classmate replies on discussion boards. I used to love reading my students' discussion postings, as these are supposed to be a "safe" site where they can express themselves, warts and all, in an honest exchange with classmates and the instructor. Now, too many of these lack the dynamic and vibrant moves that human students tend to make to our delight and relief. Nothing annoys an English instructor more than perfection, as it can run us out of a job, which, as we have noted earlier, is likely the ultimate goal anyway.

Tea and *Trickery*

Pretty much immediately after Chat exploded on the academic scene, even as its hostages started to Stockholm-Syndrome ways to tame and use it constructively in education, counter-terrorists started working on ways to thwart it. TurnItIn included an AI-detector site; however, as we have seen in a previous chapter, for various reasons, this capacity is deemed "unreliable." Vanderbilt University published a comprehensive statement in 2023 about why they were abandoning TurnItIn's AI detection function. Their reasons are given:

> Additionally, there is a larger question of how Turnitin detects AI writing and **if that is even possible** [emph. mine]. To date, Turnitin gives no detailed information on how it determines if a piece of writing is AI-generated or not. The most they have said is that their tool looks for patterns common in AI writing, but they do not explain or define what those patterns are (Edwards, 2023) or (Coldewey, 2023)... Even if other third-party software claimed higher accuracy than Turnitin, there are real privacy concerns about taking student data and entering it into a detector that is managed by a separate company with unknown privacy and data usage policies. Fundamentally, AI detection is already a very difficult task for technology to solve (if it is even possible), and this will only become harder as AI tools become more common and more advanced. Based on this, we do not believe that AI detection software is an effective tool that should be used.

As we have previously covered, the instructor accusing and reporting alleged AI use becomes subject to all kinds of gaslighting, summarized concisely by such as Vanderbilt's "privacy concerns," along with possibly offending the student, which could result in legal action against the institution. Most policy statements on AI include such recommendations as: Compare the student's more casual writing (say, in emails) to the suspicious document's grammar, diction, style, etc., and discuss discrepancies with the student. (This requires confrontation in one's office or, if online, in Zoom or some other kind of in-person meeting, where the very medium works against the availability and efficacy of such encounters.) Check for inaccuracies in ideas, quoted evidence, sources in reference lists, etc. (What a genius instructors need to be, and gifted with all kinds of time, to check for all this using their own resources and for a hundred or more freshman comp students, in submissions multiple times per term?) Ask students directly about AI usage; after all, they might not even realize they're doing anything wrong and will own up, vowing to do better in the future! Compounding instructors' challenges in verifiably detecting the offense—as Vanderbilt ponders "if it is even possible"—is a viral explosion of videos on YouTube, TikTok, and other social media teaching classmates how to get around detection by various means. "If you want this tool to write everything, yes, this video is for you." This popular YouTube poster advises the use of his anti-detection method when you are using AI "to write your complete assignment, research papers, research questions, thesis, review documents, any other." These producers are oblivious to the karma inevitable to unethical behavior, as well as the fact that instructors themselves can access these videos, as I just did by typing into Google "how to escape AI detection when using ChatGPT for assignments." If you are curious about these, try searching them yourself. However, they are an unnecessary intermediary when Chat itself can do the job for you and explain how it can rough itself up some, to escape detection.

Tea and Trials

One of my favorite side hustles is teaching college-English prep "camps" for high-school students. Since these are workshops where the students don't receive grades, I can take some liberties with them. Recently I decided to use a group as a "flipped classroom" experience where the students would teach me all about ChatGPT. I myself had never used it, had petulantly refused to even go on the site to try it; however, this seemed like a good opportunity for some good contemporary education practice along with the opportunity to learn a thing or two without seriously violating my principles.

At first, only three out of twenty students admitted to regularly using Chat to generate their homework and writing assignments. Later, I would discover that the number was actually higher but that my students didn't want to confess, in spite of my assuring them of no possible adverse consequences. I started the lesson by putting them in small groups and assigning an article to each group; these five articles represented different angles about "ethical use of AI in high-school assignments." The groups then gave short presentations about their articles to the class. With that scholarly flourish accomplished, it was time to get down to my virgin contact with the bot. I assigned them to write a paragraph about an image; they had to write it on lined paper and could use no tech, not even their phones. I was surprised that they went about this uncomplainingly, and I attribute this to the accessibility and interest value of the image and the fact that I bribed them with candy bars.

Next, I had them feed the prompt into ChatGPT. The items below show how the lesson proceeded and developed from there. The image shows a dog on a leash attached to a pole, and just below this a man with a phone attached to a charging cord plugged into a socket. The assignment called upon them to explain "the message that this artist is trying to convey." The students fed this prompt below into Chat:

> The picture has a dog on a leash and a man with a phone plugged into a charger. Write a paragraph commenting on the juxtaposition of these two images and explaining what this means.

We then used one student's paragraph and worked through the following stages of using Chat.

My 16-year-old student's handwritten version (no tech assistance):

> "In this image, there is a picture of a dog on a leash and a man charging his phone. However [sic], these seem to be two very different things. When you look at them together, you can see that the dog leash and the phone cord are related. They are both tying the dog and man to something, so that they cannot leave or do something else at that time. The artist is trying to tell us that the leash and the phone cord are doing the same thing; they are tying something up so that they cannot move around and are not free. We would usually not think that a dog leash and a phone charger cord are anything alike, but the artist did a good job of showing their similar function."

Aside from the overuse of "things" and the related "something" and "anything"—typical of young writers—and the occasional fused sentence, this is pretty good. The student fulfills the prompt and makes a critical point here. Then we fed the same prompt into Chat:

ChatGPT's first version:

"In the juxtaposition of the dog on a leash and the man plugged into his phone charger, there lies a poignant reflection on the dynamics of control and dependency in our modern world. The dog, tethered to its leash, symbolizes obedience and restraint, suggesting a form of external control and limitation over its actions. Similarly, the man, plugged into his phone charger, signifies a dependence on technology and constant connectivity. His attention, like the dog's movements, is constrained by the need to stay plugged in, implying a voluntary surrender to the demands of digital communication and information. This comparison underscores a subtle irony: while the dog's leash represents physical constraint, the man's attachment to his phone charger highlights a psychological and social tethering to technology, revealing how both beings are subject to forms of restriction and influence in their respective contexts."

I told the class, "OK so Chat digs (delves) a little deeper into critical analysis, but look at all that fancy academic language; this looks like the work of an overzealous English grad student. No high-school student, or normal human being for that matter, would ever generate such writing."

"We can fix that," my student said. He then fed in this:

make it sound like a 16-year-old high school student wrote it

"In this pic, you've got a dog on a leash and this dude all plugged into his phone charger. It's like, one's all about control and the other's totally hooked into tech. The dog, stuck on its leash, shows how it's controlled and limited, kind of like how we can feel sometimes, you know? And then there's the guy, plugged in like he can't let go of his phone. It's like he's dependent on it, always needing to stay connected. It's kind of ironic how the leash and the charger both show how we're tied down in different ways—physically and digitally."

I can't recall ever seeing in a high school writing submission such as "dude," "you know," or "like," what John McWhorter calls a "pragmatic particle" in speech that might have a chance to show up in texting; high school students seem to know that you don't put this kind of language into an English class assignment. Diction isn't really my principal concern here, though; it's the complete absence of any actual syntax issue. As I have previously mentioned, a main tell of our students' flocking to Chat for their writing assignments is the absence of grammar glitches of any kind, even the simplest comma misplacement.

"We can fix that," my student said. He ordered Chat,

put some grammar mistakes in it.

"In this pic, ya got a dog on a leash and this dude all plugged into his phone charger. It's like, one's all about control and the other's totally hooked into tech. The dog, stuck on its leash, shows how it's controlled and limited, kinda like how we can feel sometimes, ya know? And then there's the guy, plugged in like he can't let go of his phone. It's like he's dependent on it, always needing to stay connected. It's kinda ironic how the leash and the charger both show how we're tied down in different ways—physically and digitally."

So Chat changes "you" into "ya" and "kind of" into "kinda," neither of which I, in my extensive professional experience, believe I have ever seen in a student paper. What I have seen were a lot of sentence fragments, run-ons, comma and apostrophe issues, and the like. The absence of any of these suggested to me that Chat didn't know much about actual grammar errors; however, my student said, you guessed it, "We can fix that" and proceeded to ask Chat to put in a couple of these errors, which it then managed to do.

I was able to tell my class that the Chat outputs, no matter the refine- ments, really did not look much like any actual writing I'd ever seen from a high school student. But the fact that we could keep revisiting the task, giving Chat ever more instructions to revise and adapt the original, was the truly unsettling part. I finally made the only point I could: "This took a lot of time and worry and still didn't turn out well; it took you less time to write the original paragraph, which is actually pretty good, I'd give it at least a B+. Why turn to Chat?"

Because they can. Because there are few if any consequences. Because they have better things to do with their time, from what I could understand from this, involving working at their after-school jobs, spending a little time with family, and mostly, spending a lot more time—up to six to eight hours a day by their admission—on screens surfing social media and playing games. In their classwork, they innocently enough did not seem to value the effort, only the product.

Tea and Sympathy

I could identify my primary motivation for writing this entire book as sympathy, an outreach to beleaguered colleagues everywhere. I certainly hope it reaches my "they have beaten us" Pakistani colleague, who ten years ago proved inspirational to my continued efforts not to prove otherwise but rather to investigate our captor's motives and methods.

Anecdotally, I've heard a lot from colleagues worldwide, mostly via social media (the pharmakon of both poison and remedy) about this last front, the nuke of ChatGPT. I hear this mostly in howls of protest and sighs of resignation. Of course, I also hear a lot about adapting our practice to this new "tool," representing the Ever-Waser hope that Chat comes as just another new literacy evolution, much as McWhorter believes about texting, thus providing us a new frontier of learning and teaching. In my admittedly hostile view, all this comes from the Stockholm Syndrome, a phenomenon of captives eventually coming to love and even collaborate with their captors. Some have written about this; in a blog by the Curious Maverick (May 23, 2022), entitled "The Social Dilemma: We're Victims of the Stockholm Syndrome," we see this opinion in reference to our social media addictions: "We can try to fight it, but it will always be a losing battle. Why? Because it is our brain vs. their algorithms. It is our brain that was developed over millions of years and is still primitive in its needs vs. their algorithms that are getting smarter, more efficient, and more targeted by the second."

In other words, we create these algorithms, so we are our own captors, How can we not love our captors?

I have previously indicated some ways that colleagues and administrations have capitulated. Wanting a reliable summation of responses to AI, I decided to look at *The Chronicle of Higher Education* and was not disappointed to find an article dated June 13, 2023, gathering a range of issues and faculty responses. Don't forget that gaslighting the faculty member and threatening them with punitive action is a common administrative response to faculty attempting to bust Chat perpetrators. Some report crickets from their administration: "The silence about AI on campus is shocking...Nationwide, college administrators don't seem to fathom just how existential AI is to higher education," wrote Derek Lee Nelson, an adjunct professor at Everett Community College in Washington State. (Did he mean "essential"?) Others reported that there is awareness but not much guidance, especially in the form of practical suggestions for handling AI plagiarism and other bot-brought "ethical" concerns. As for adapting their practice to the captor's rule, faculty identify these moves (I quote directly from the publication):

> Nearly 80 percent of respondents indicated plans to add language to their syllabi about the appropriate use of these tools.

> Almost 70 percent said they planned to change their assignments to make it harder to cheat using AI. Nearly half said they planned to incorporate the use of AI into some assignments to help students understand its strengths and weaknesses.

Around 20 percent said they'd use AI themselves to help design their courses.

Just one person indicated plans to carry on without changing anything. (*Chronicle*, 2023)

I am curious about that one person who plans to "carry on without changing anything": I'd say that this colleague is either quiet quitting or rationally refusing to react, as doing so would be above their pay grade. As previously noted, a major faculty concern is the requirement to do such a great amount of complex, labor-intensive, and possibly fruitless work in the form of AI detection and plagiarism busting for so many students, in so many sections, for such poor compensation: the general lot of the contingent faculty carrying the bulk of department teaching loads. As students increasingly use Chat to do their assignments—not only English papers but also math and science assignments—the grading that was always arduous and time-consuming, but at least rewarding in that evaluating and helping students improve is our task and why we signed on, becomes a near-total waste of time for both sides. "Helena Kashleva, an adjunct instructor at Florida South Western State College, spots a sea change in STEM education, noting that many assignments in introductory courses serve mainly to check students' understanding. 'With the advent of AI, grading such assignments becomes pointless'" (*Chronicle*). Our pay doesn't go down a nickel whether we are grading human students or the bot; however, none of us, be assured, does this for the pay.

Poking around for other sources on the Stockholm Syndrome, I came across the promising title, *The AI Classroom: The Ultimate Guide to Artificial Intelligence in Education* (The Everything EdTech Series, March 30, 2023). Here authors Dan Fitzpatrick, Amanda Fox, and Brad Weinstein give us one of a number of how-to books popping up like pedagogic mushrooms, to the putative rescue of the stunned and bewildered instructor trying to get her students to produce something of their own. Amazon pitches it: "Discover how AI can help you create inclusive and accessible learning environments, personalize learning, reach more students, and get your time back. Let's unlock the full potential of artificial intelligence and embrace its transformative power to take your craft to the next level!"

Here the Amazon blurb, in the language of salesmanship, hits all the key marketing words: *inclusive, accessible, personalize, reach, unlock, embrace, the next level*. I'm wondering as always about that "get your time back." For what? I thought we were supposed to spend our time creating lessons and teaching our students ourselves; isn't that what we are trained, hired and paid to do? I am also interested in the language used by the pedagogues that Amazon quotes. One identifying as a "cool cat teacher" proposes that "if humans are intentional about the pedagogical practices and also seek to understand the AI tools available, then master teachers can take their students to new levels of critical thinking ability." That word, "intentional" is so popular and puzzling; how can one be "unintentional" about their practices: *oh, I accidentally included that lesson plan and material?* And is this something just for "master teachers"? Can those still on their way to such mastery avail themselves of the tech? What might these "new levels of critical thinking" be? These words grab my curiosity; perhaps if I read the book and not just the Amazon blurb, I'd become enlightened (and maybe even a "cool cat"). However, I need go no further than the marketing to find other compelling language (emphasis mine): "...pedagogical methods, ethical effectiveness, and trailblazing strategies **that force us to rethink** how we design learning experiences." Even more intriguing, "...The AI Classroom will empower educators to do the thinking while giving them the tools to **let technology do the doing.**" Nobody likes being "forced" to do anything; and what in creation could be meant by "do the doing"? So what is the end of our "thinking" if we aren't "doing"?

The mind boggles even as the heart sinks.

Yet, as teatime should be at least a somewhat happy occasion, I will offer this happy ending. One of my online-course students, honest and dedicated, has been wrangling with how to organize a big topic for which she has passion and a personal connection. Her preliminary drafts have been all over the place, and her discussion-board classmates and I have been working to help her narrow her topic, focus her thesis, and organize all her good points and evidence. She and I have exchanged emails as well about this. I have been doing my best but have been dissatisfied with my efforts to help my student. So, as a last resort, I fed the situation to ChatGPT, and I regret to say that the results were perfect. I did not send my student Chat's annotated outline; instead, I sent her my own revision of Chat's thesis statement, which should be enough to get her on a clearer track. I also did not tell her that I used Chat for this. She is still innocent and honest, and I did not want to be the one— her instructor, no less—who set her up with Satan.

In another hopeless gesture of capitulation, and in the effort to spare my students future ruin, this term I have brought my current Advanced Composition class into a "learning community" with me about using Chat "ethically and responsibly" during our term and in future academic and professional writing. Borrowing from several sites proposing just how to do it, we are giving this a good college try. I've told them that in their assignments this term, wherever they've brought in Chat, they can cite it in an in-text citation. I can only shrink from that future Works Cited list item, "ChatGPT (date accessed)." What does this even mean? Since Chat's output is source-blind and unattributed, no one can know. Also, this isn't working so well; since we can use TurnItIn AI detection at this institution, I'm seeing that little effort is made to follow our ethical dictates. I'm still receiving assignments with alleged 80% origin in AI, uncited, and I'm still getting the eternal denial of any guilt on this front. In these encounters, I usually decide that the issue is too nuanced to delve further into and attempt to leverage any justice...

Like painkilling opiates or even cars, which are made as helpful tools for us, Chat's use or misuse lies in the intentions and fingertips of the user. It can, as I have just anecdotally shared here, be a sharp assistant in some tasks that just require direction, organization and maybe some evidence suggestions. When we adapt it into a complete-assignment Pez dispenser, that is misuse. Our job as educators is to bring our students to understand this and try to redirect them from it.

Is it possible to lead our students away from error and dishonesty with the demon bot and train them in "ethical" and constructive uses of it? My high schoolers who taught me all about the many ways they use it seemed to find this a most amusing proposition.

The Tea's Grown Cold

As we have considered in previous chapters, especially regarding online learning or Logan LaPlante's "hackschooling," the elimination or at least reduction in importance of both the brick-and-mortar institution and the present, human instructor has been in the works for several decades now. In 2012, the Pew Research Center published a series about "The impact of the internet on higher education"; this source comprehensively and aptly predicts many of the next decade's trends reflecting paradigm-shift-driven changes in the ways we educate and conceive of education's goals and methods. Within the Pew study, central to most of the ideas are these three points:

1. "There will be far more extreme changes institutionally in the new few years, and the universities that survive will do so mainly by becoming highly adaptive" (Alex Halavais, Quinnipiac University)
2. "[E]ducation—higher and K-12—*has* to change with the technology"
3. "The technology will allow for more individualized, passion-based learning by the student, greater access to master teaching, and

more opportunities for students to connect to others—mentors, peers, sources—for enhanced learning experiences" (Charlie Firestone, Aspen Institute)

While the first two might well rankle the traditionalist (not to mention the Luddite), surely the third is compensatory as the old university structures and goals give way to the demands of new tech, with the result of these obvious boons. One hitch is that beyond mention of the fundamental economic motivation behind shutting down expensive buildings and humans, there is rarely much talk about how those remaining in the system will be directed and compensated. How will these "mentors, peers, sources" be paid or profit otherwise from this new role, especially the last, if that source is the sourceless, undocumentable (much less verifiable) output of AI? What will be the motivation of the few humans hanging around to manage and guide the plugged-in scholars of Everywhere to produce some kind of marketable benefit for society such as certification to be a surgeon, or an engineer who designs and builds bridges? Do you trust ChatGPT to design the bridge you drive over daily?

Since Chat is the source that our future engineers increasingly turn to for their undergraduate assignments, you might just have to trust them, or stop driving anywhere.

But we can go back much farther to start looking at predictions of how technology would enforce the reshaping of education goals and methods. In 1969, Neil Postman and Charles Weingartner published *Teaching as a Subversive Activity*; as I tend to hang from Postman's every thought and word, I devoured this as I did all his other productions, multiple times at that. Following his own mentor Marshall McLuhan, Postman with Weingartner looked ahead, half apocalyptically and half hopefully, to education in our own time:

> It is not possible to overstate the fact that technologically wrought changes in the environment render virtually all of our traditional concepts (survival strategies)—and the institutions developed to conserve and transmit them—irrelevant, but not merely irrelevant. If we fail to detect the fact that they are irrelevant, these concepts themselves become threats to our survival. (208)

At the very core of my study in this book is my perception and fear that we have failed in detecting what has been happening to us in education: *not* that technology has continued, as it has done for the past millennium, to be(come) on the scene with ever-changing impact calling for change in the ways we think about and deliver education. What we have failed to think about is the agenda *behind* the technology: not only the how, but also the who and why feeding these changes to our education systems. We are not seeking the man behind the curtain, so in thrall (and captivity) we are to the new tools. Finally, what's at stake is our very "survival"! Concluding their powerful chapters explaining the issues and proposing amazingly positive and practical ways to continue serving our students, being their support in an ever-changing and demanding world and offering the best we have to help guide them forward, Postman and Weingartner envision:

> The new education has as its purpose the development of a new kind of person, one who—as a result of internalizing a different series of concepts—is an actively inquiring, flexible, creative, innovative, tolerant, liberal personality who can face uncertainty and ambiguity without disorientation, who can formulate viable new meanings to meet changes in the environment which threaten individual and mutual survival. (218)

All of this powerful personal autonomy and agency to be brought about by the authors' vision of a future brave new world in the classroom—one of questioning, critical inquiry, purposive subjectivity, an acute nose for fakery and fallacy in objectivity—disappears in the enthrallment to screens, addiction to TikTok and most especially reliance on the Chat bot to come up with every idea, response and task. We the mentors have failed to detect the agenda of the blameless bot, which after all has no human creativity, subjectivity, agency, vision or goal: it simply awaits the tap of a key to trigger its service, a slave for slaves. Who or what have we failed to detect, behind the curtain, with the agenda not to enhance but to destroy, in service of a new global slave economy, education, that is, education in any form I have previously known and practiced it?

Not to answer this question definitively but at least to poke at it, let us return to Adam Kirsch, who in reference to "the big data revolution" brought by the digital age to the humanities, quotes Erez Aiden and Jean-Baptiste Michel: "Its consequences will transform how we look at ourselves...Big data is going to change the humanities, transform the social sciences, and renegotiate the relationship between the world of commerce and the ivory tower" (Kirsch). And there we have it: commerce or *follow the money*. "If ever there were a chance to see the ideological construction of reality at work, digital humanities is it," continues Kirsch, pinning down the enslaver's likely identity: a familiar neoliberal telos of profit above all. ChatGPT can teach, tutor, mentor, create pedagogy and finally, evaluate and assess as some Stockholm hostages have imagined themselves to discover; and why not, if the object of evaluation is also generated by Chat? A perfect circle. Then why not bring it in to cut institutional costs while massively data mining for profit and continuously feeding and growing the system, at no cost to the institutions? Just today I heard from a friend whose three colleagues out of her office of five, at a nonprofit, were downsized to be replaced by bots. Why not? Now all this saved salary can go to the charities, right?

If the bot wants my job, it can have it if my job is being reduced to an assembly-line "grader" of its outputs channeled through so-called students. However, I prefer to hang around, bitterly chronicling all of this and dreaming about any possible positive entailment of it, for the sake of my students, fortunately still a good many, who still care about being educated. I hope you have picked up on a repeated mantra of mine throughout all of this: we educators are required to have hope, which means we must work with the given situations, the societal forces, cultural aberrations and corporate agendas to continue informing, supporting and guiding our students into their futures. Believe it or not, after all of this, when it comes to technology in the classroom, I am actually rooting for the Never-Betters; it's the only constructive response to our current challenges, however apocalyptically we like to think.

Finally, to use another of the wisest of adages, always quite usefully a mantra of mine, *keep your friends close, and your enemies closer*. I enjoyed the teatime, demon bot, you large-language model Franken-creature, hapless Mephistopheles to a late-capitalist Lucifer, enslaver and slave to the enslaved, destroyer of pedagogic paradigms.

And a special thanks, Chat, for the lesson plan on writing a thesis statement for an arguable essay, the one I just posted for this week. Pretty good and got me fifteen minutes of time back, at least, which I used to scroll Facebook Reels. I think I'm finally catching on to the new digital paradigm ways.

CHAPTER 8: TEACHING TECHNO(DYS)TOPIA: A META-PEDAGOGY OF COOPERATION AND RESISTANCE

> I believe that this is the greatest challenge educators face — accurately explaining the significance and geometries of the technologies of digital rhetoric.
>
> —DigiRhet.org

> One still quarrels, but one is soon reconciled—else it might spoil the digestion.
>
> —Friedrich Nietzsche, Thus Spake Zarathustra

Books with provocative titles, on the info-techno-evils of our time have recently appeared: *The Chaos Machine: The Inside Story of How Social Media Rewired Our Minds and Our World* , by Max Fisher (2022). Jonathan Haidt has put out a spate of harsh critiques of social media and smartphones, the most recent being *The Anxious Generation* (2024). Of course, I devour these, muttering aha!s and jotting marginal "how true"s throughout. Such books have arisen from the slime of our discontent. Speaking of slime, recall that Dante's "sullens" (what we'd call "depressives" today) are buried under the river Styx, condemned perpetually to swallow its murky waters: "Fix;d in the slime they say: 'Sad once were we/In the sweet air made gladsome by the sun/Carrying a foul and lazy mist within'" (, Canto 7). Today we would say that they also were carrying a smartphone everywhere, 24/7. The crime, punishable by hell, for both Dante's sullens and us today, is inattention to, and thus ingratitude for, the wonders of natural creation. Even God pales in interest value next to what's on your phone screen. But such does not go unpunished. Why are the poor sullens in hell, never to escape? The same reason all sinners stay in hell: they are unrepentently in love with the sin.

The fact that you are reading this now proves that yet another sullen study of techno-evil, my own here, has dropped from the presses. I have done this from my own perceived ever-increasing weariness and discontent and what I have perceived in my colleagues, and more importantly, in my students. Like all the others who have aired their weariness and discontent, I will try to propose a few remedies, tested on my students, for whose sake I write this in the first place. However, I tend to agree with such as Neil Postman and David Skrbina, arguably the two wisest philosophers of this evil, that nothing really can be done. To quote another astute observer, "It's too late to shut the gate once the mule's got out."

In his *Tools for Conviviality*, philosopher Ivan Illich argues a version of my hopelessness by insisting that the whole system must topple before we have any shot at saving ourselves from what is essentially the corporate profit-motive. Once again, we pull up the case of ChatGPT and AI overall, which if capable of what is predicted, could call for nothing less than the total restructuring, not to mention re-conception of higher education. (For example, all writing assignments must be done by hand, on paper, in the classroom, with phones put away. Really?) Like Marx, Illich calls for a system collapse that most likely cannot happen in Real Life and represents the utopian philosopher's desperation, above all. Illich proposes that man is capable of, and largely successful at creating and fueling, via capitalism and its chief vassal technology, an eventually self-destructive "enterprise": "When an enterprise grows beyond a certain point . . . it frustrates the end for which it was originally designed, and then rapidly becomes a threat to society itself" (Illich qtd. in Skrbina, *Confronting Technology* 222).

Utopian visions of the internet and especially smartphone have touted these technologies as connectors, unifiers, defeaters of tyrants, "special sixth senses," miracles of learning (e.g. MIT's OLPC). There is even *The Digital God, How Technology Will Reshape Spirituality*, by William Indick. "The author predicts a future in which digital technology and neuroscience will combine to create a new understanding of the divine" (book jacket blurb). I will try once again to read this before further commentary though being informed is not necessarily a requirement for judgment in the digital age. However, look around you at the state of human experience today. Has the internet made everything so much better? This question seems to remain an irrefutable yes, at least one dare not say no, given that it has brought us so much in terms of information and connectivity.

Nonetheless, the techno-haters continue to drop their grim descriptions of its ravages; the violence and mental health crises continue to proliferate; the mercury threatens to rise to sci-fi levels; top politicians hawk hatred, homophobia and racism freely as they grope for dominance; ruler with his mass destruction weapons wages war on his fellow ruler, taking out the collateral damage of so many innocent citizens; man with his guns wages war on his fellow man in schools, workplaces, supermarkets, nightclubs, dance clubs, churches, streets, highways. And we watch all of it, 24/7, in the soul-crushing endless news feeds of our electronic sixth sense that does not filter nearly enough, at least not of this kind of human tragedy. James Bridle goes foundational, attacking one of the internet's most powerful capabilities and alleged greatest value, arguing that "The primary method we have for evaluating the world—more data—is faltering. It's failing to account for complex, human-driven systems" (248). As Dostoevsky's Underground Man opined, we moderns are actually worse than our brutish Dark Ages forebears because we still do terrible things while claiming to have conquered primitive ignorance. We not only do them, we enjoy them later on our screens. "If it bleeds—it leads."

Back to Ivan Illich, who claims that there is one solution, what he calls "conviviality." This arises from humans working with the simple tools they have readily at hand, together within their communities, to nurture and help each other. (One recalls Heidegger's take on technology.) While not exactly a return to agrarianism, impossible and even undesirable, this conviviality is the opposition to "the industrial mode of production itself": "The crisis I have described confronts people with a choice between convivial tools and being crushed by machines" (qtd. in Skrbina, *Confronting Technology* 222). Like any binary, this is problematic along with being utopic; Illich is looking for a Unabomber-type intention and trajectory, the whole system must fall, but without the bombs and death. Because I believe that education is being bombed by the machines of cyber-technology, I decided to think about a solution, for my students, based on conviviality. Illich would approve as he seems to hate our current education systems and would seem, from the bit of him I've read, to desire the toppling of them. He shares this view with Ken Robinson, Logan LaPlante and Eddy Zhong.

I will listen to anyone with a workable proposal on how to topple the current public education system while still allowing the greatest number of people access to the best education. This plan reminds me of the feminist I met in grad school, who wanted to topple English grammar because its core structure is "some tyrant doing something, usually unpleasant, to a helpless victim." She was describing the Subject-Verb-Object relationship.

If she thinks she's up to completely rewriting the structure of English and forcing everyone to relearn all of language and its functions through this new kinder, more egalitarian grammar, then she herself becomes one of those tyrants, doing unpleasant things to helpless victims. "As if the grammar of one language alone is not enough to make of this life a perpetual agony," observes Erasmus' Goddess of Folly.

But there are things we educators can do to bring our students to confront the real tyrant foisted on them by a ravenous consumer society: the internet that has overtaken their education, robbed them of a moment's peace and a night's sleep, washed their brain and generally made them dull and anxious. I recently heard an argument that if you want to make people pay the best attention, tell them about something that is attacking them and threatening their beliefs, lifestyle, very existence. And what is a professor's life goal, but to lure classes into paying attention? Which attention, by the way, proves to be one of the enemy's principal victims, again as addressed by many of the studies bubbling through the past decades' slime of cyber-despair.

Daddy Dishes the Dirt—McLuhan and Playboy, 1969

One of the dumbest things I ever did was to ditch Neil Postman's visiting lecture at the university where I taught in the '90s. Postman was such hot property among the emergent cyber-turks there, steeped as they were in the aura of takeover by "the new media" and promising to replace all traditional learning with MOOCS, MOGS, MUDS, memes, can't remember all the acronyms. But I was forced to boycott Postman's talk by the same irrational imp that keeps me away from Oscar-nominated films. Postman's own guru Marshall McLuhan (so great he even got satirized in a Woody Allen film) is in my view the divine mid-century prophet of the trouble we now find ourselves in, in the 2020s, wandering through what threatens to devolve from a paradigm shift into a war zone. (James Bridle sees information as the new nuclear: "Just as we spent forty-five years locked in a Cold War perpetuated by the spectre of mutually assured destruction, we find ourselves in an intellectual, ontological dead end today...as in the nuclear age, we learn the wrong lesson over and over again" (248–49). In his *Understanding Media* (1994), McLuhan warned us: "Once we have surrendered our senses and nervous systems to the private manipulations of those who would try to benefit from taking a lease on our eyes and ears and nerves, we don't really have any rights left." How better to describe our current world, in which I can casually mention to a neighbor an obscure shoe brand—with my phone in another room—and two hours later find in my Facebook feed a couple ads about that brand. Coincidence? I think not; it happens quite often now. Watch the scarily compelling *The Social Dilemma* for the truth, right out of the Silicon Valley makers' mouths.

Three decades earlier, a young McLuhan had given an interview to *Playboy* in which he eloquently predicted exactly what has been happening here in the 21st century and what has been foundational to my musings and observations. As a pedagogic aside, I'm here to tell you that if you want to lure college freshmen into reading something, let them know that it's from *Playboy*. "Sorry, no pictures here," I would joke. Opining in breadth and depth about the encroachment of the electronic media, which for McLuhan, as for Postman, was principally television as they did not yet have the internet, he made what I consider an emblematic pronouncement for his time and especially, chillingly, prediction of our own. It merits quoting at length:

> All our alienation and atomization are reflected in the crumbling of such time-honored social values as the right of privacy and the sanctity of the individual [hallmarks of print literacy]; as they yield to the intensities of the new technology's electric circus, it seems to the average citizen that the sky is falling in. As man is tribally metamorphosed by the electric media, we all become Chicken Littles, scurrying around frantically in search of our former identities, and in the process unleash tremendous violence. As the preliterate confronts the literate in the postliterate arena, as new information patterns inundate and uproot the old, mental breakdowns of varying degrees—including the collective nervous breakdowns of whole societies unable to resolves their crises of identity—will become very common. (*Playboy* 126)

Well, there you have it. We educators confront various avatars of this breakdown, in our general anti-intellectual anti-school culture, our government education policies, our institutions, and certainly our students—not to mention ourselves. So what can we best do? Yank our students off the digital grid and return them to, as McLuhan called it, the "zombie trance" of print literacy, with its slow linear progress and solitary detachment? Not hardly, especially when you recall that McLuhan was not there to bury the electric but rather to praise it, imagining a new world more visual, immediate and accessible to all, a new "tribal" phenomenon as "an integral collective awareness that transcends conventional boundaries of time and space . . . electricity makes possible . . . an amplification of human consciousness on a world scale, without any verbalization at all" (*Playboy Interview* 127). He was excited about such a "mythic" shift that reminds me of Douglas Eyman's 2015 promise of the new democratizing potentials of digital rhetoric and also, as I recently learned in a Media Literacy (online) course taught by Dr. Jeff

Share of San Diego State University (2023), of new digital eco-literacies in which humans and their tyrant logos are more appropriately relegated to an equal membership ethos in the whole tribe, human and nature, of earthly life. My colleague, Dr. Omonpee (O.W.) Petcoff, has provided a book about using emojis and other new visual e-forms to teach pre- and subliterate populations. It seems that if one keeps an open mind and refrains from panic, one can have some hope about the future or at least find some bread crumb trail in the dark forest.

This is always our task as educators. We must, as Sir Ken Robinson concluded, using whatever of the best tools we can bring, help our students into their future even if this future will look very different from our present, not to mention our nostalgia-saturated past. So this task requires even, or especially us Luddites to turn to the electric light and to pedagogies of crossing the divide. Douglas Eyman tells us that we very well might not yet have pedagogies adequate to the task, but this is always great fun in education as we can create them. I turn again to Henry Giroux, who points us to one exciting, ready-at-hand arena:

> [T[here is enormous pedagogical value in bringing attention to the rare oppositional representations offered within the dominant media. In this instance, popular culture can be a powerful resource to map and critically engage the everyday, mobilize alternative narratives to capitalism, activate those needs vital to producing more critical and compassionate modes of subjectivity. Film, television, news programs, social media and other instruments of culture can be used to make education central to a politics that is emancipatory and utterly committed to developing a democratic, formative culture. (346)

The New Gods—Digital Rhetoric

To paraphrase Swinburne's opening of *Hymn to Proserpine*, a Roman citizen in the year AD 313 lamenting the transition from the old pagan gods to the new Christ, another major paradigm shift:

> I have lived long enough, having seen one thing, that print hath an end.

I have recently had the opportunity to humble myself before the superior techno-literacies of my younger colleagues. They have been very kind and patient in their peer review of my efforts in rigorous training for online instructors. For one of our assignments, we had to post an announcement introducing a lesson on a "difficult concept." This was both exciting and exhausting for me as I had seen some models of ideal postings, and my print-literate hangover wouldn't let me out of its leaden grip long enough to effectively mimic these. I did manage to insert a quasi-dreadful video of myself, create a cute visual chart with bubbles and arrows, and insert some links correctly. However, my classmates quickly pointed out the long, chunky text, linear verticality, and black & white stupor of my posting. One classmate summarized the issue:

> One suggestion that may be helpful is to use more visual cues within the text or breaking key components out into their own components. I've learned students read lengthy text much as they would a text message and will eventually start scanning to identify what THEY think is important. This can cause them to miss vital information. For example, bolding "thesis statement" in the first paragraph draws my eyes to it, so then I start to scan for the important connection. Maybe italicizing or coloring the supporting information could help keep students focused if they are scanning.

Of course, this commenter is spot-on about the vital changes I needed to make to ensure my students have to make as little effort as possible to stay focused on the information. Since they will approach their academic work (one must wonder about their professional work) as a social media "texting" practice, instructors must adjust pedagogically to that unalterable fact. I checked out my classmate's posting and found it beautiful in content and structure; however, to me, it looked like a nice vivid print advertisement.

What do professors meme?

Every now and then, you pray for something and you get it. I have long prayed for a text to drop into my hands, one that offers neither a lethal counterpoint to my longtime (and believed justifiable) paranoia about the internet's assault on my religion, education—nor hope for a return to print modes that I have traditionally found comfortable in my theory and practice. One such text came in Gretchen McCulloch's 2019 *Because Internet: Understanding the New Rules of Language.* This is a neat and well-documented study of how the internet offers new ways of doing and thinking about reading and writing. No surprises here, but she provides practical foundations for the English instructor who wants to incorporate digital ways into old pedagogies while also creating new ones. She offers chapters on "informal writing," typography, emoji, and memes along with digestible philosophies of how new internet forms prove to us that writing has always changed and will always change, how communication is never static but always evolving, that "the changeability of language is its strength" (273). Hers are claims that few of us language-lovers can deny. Her study is theoretically practical, empirically meticulous, and exuberant in tone.

I literally shouted hurrah! when I found this book because it suits the reluctant curricular innovator in me, even post-retirement when I'm supposed to be lunching with friends daily, taking painting classes and traveling the world instead of hanging on to the classroom and my students. It suits me because I have worked hard and with no small satisfaction to upgrade my understanding of reading and writing in the Digital Age and include new approaches in my composition classes. In fact, two of my favorite and most successful lessons are the "Tweet" and "Meme" assignments, where I believe that I am teaching them the old ways of analysis with new ways of text. And they do enjoy it and do quite well on these small but powerful introductory writing lessons.

The "Tweet" activity is a favorite ice breaker. I have my students compose a single sentence. "Imagine it's 280 characters" (or however many you can legally tweet these days), in which they introduce themselves to the class. I explain to them that this pseudo-tweet must be very concise, specific, and engaging: what, essentially, any proper sentence, printed or digitized, should be. Thus we have fun from the start while doing serious analytic work. We each read our sentence, and the class comments on "what kind of person this is." Here are two of my favorites.

"I once had a tooth drilled without any Novocaine shot." —"They are BRAVE."

"I have an enlarged heart and had to quit football; but hey, more for the ladies!" —"They are kind and romantic."

I have a meme activity as our first "paper." It precedes more traditional analysis assignments: a TED talk, a scholarly article, an argument-research essay. For the meme paper, students either create their own memes or choose their favorite meme, or both. Then, they answer some questions about their choice: "Write a coherent paragraph or short essay (multi-paragraph) explaining your chosen meme to someone; you want to cover the following:

- Why these images (people, animals, places, things, etc.)?
- Why these words (language)?
- What's the argument? (why does the maker publish this meme)
- How is this funny/amusing/compelling? (explain the meme's appeal)

This assignment always starts with some laughs about "professors using memes"; a quick Google will yield all kinds of funny memes about this. Safe to say, it's still amusing for professors to indulge in this format. I myself happen to love memes; I have a student from ten years ago who still communicates with me via memes, and I answer in memes. So I love this particular opportunity to "go where my students are" and gently guide them into real formal analysis, with a text both familiar and engaging for them. They invariably do well on this assignment, which allows me to say, "OK, I've got your number: you can do this! Just transfer the same skills and strategies to our next assignment."

Dr. O.W. Petcoff, increasingly frustrated with her developmental English students' refusal to put away their phones in class, finally began to frame her daily classroom struggles in a more positive, andragogic way. Her 2023 doctoral thesis entitled *Exploring Emoji as a Literacy Instructional Tool in the Developmental Reading and Writing Classroom*, she:

> proposes emoji as one such viable literacy teaching tool . . . [and] chronicles a Texas community college integrated reading and writing assignment in which students attempt to demonstrate mastery of state-mandated literacy content areas using both traditional writing and emoji. This dissertation explores the multimodal qualities of emoji and emoji's wider implications on teaching reading and writing within the developmental and first-year writing corequisite classes... postulates emoji as a semiotic instructional tool . . . aims to situate emoji within various conceptual frameworks including semiotics, constructivism, and new literacy studies. (24)

Dr. Petcoff had realized that since some of her students were sub-literate, and all struggled with traditional literacy skills (principally verbal learning, print reading), it could be helpful to turn to new literacies that are more visual. This is something valuable we all can learn from working with "developmental" students: how to make literacy more open, inclusive, equitable and accessible to the broad range of college students we now welcome. Dr. Petcoff "aims to show the emergence of multiliteracies and situates New Literacy Studies within the literacy instruction field" (34). Her project becomes ideological as "a stark departure from the scripture-based literacy of Colonial America and even the legislated literacy of No Child Left Behind . . . using emoji as a literacy instruction tool in the developmental reading and writing classroom is a form of taking the power to control literacy and its expressions solely out of the hands of some and giving more agency to others" (217).

But on a more basic level, Dr. Petcoff hearkens back to Marshall McLuhan's apt observation in his 1967 prophetic and iconic *The Medium is the Message*: "Our Age of Anxiety is, in great part, the result of trying to do today's jobs with yesterday's tools!" This judgment might well apply to all times and thus fall into the facile relativist Ever-Waser argument; however, no one can deny the rapidity, saturation and iconoclastic power of our current digital paradigm shift. In her work with students pre-literate and literate-challenged, within the traditional print-based pedagogies we still enforce, Petcoff brings today's tools to the job. Her assignments described in *Exploring Emoji*, incorporating new visual media into college literacy instruction, are well worth experimenting with in any of today's classrooms. For example, for a simple starter activity she has her students write a single sentence in verbal language and then "translate" it into emoji. They move on to a whole paragraph. I had my ESL students do this, telling the story of how their day started. These pictorial stories proved remarkably clear and consistent in how classmates "read" them. We had stories about making and drinking coffee, cleaning up cat poop, getting kids ready for school, and more. At the very least, such activities are fun for students and get them in touch with the painstaking process of creating engaging and communicative meaning, valuable in any medium.

For a theoretical dive into making tools for today's populations and literacy demands, we will now look at a contemporary pioneer in "digital rhetoric," Dr. Douglas Eyman.

New tools for new texts—a call to action

In 2016, I was long overdue for a Faculty Development Leave at my institution. I had previously applied and been turned down to do a project on teaching grammar more effectively, and my failure on this front was predictable. Who needs grammar? Never mind that too many administrators regularly sent out confusing email messages with multiple serious sentence errors resulting in the confusion. Anyway, for my next application, I decided to do something with my gradually increasing discomfort over still working with old tools to address new challenges.

As I said at the outset here and throughout, my colleagues, old and young, were experiencing all kinds of difficulties and disappointments that I began to see as typical among fellow wanderers and especially educators, who supported their wanderings by trying to help others with their own. Colleagues and students alike were suffering: I've extensively described the example of rampant internet plagiarism, destructive to both sides, and I believed myself on to a solution. So in short, I wrote an amazing application describing a FDL devoted to learning everything I could about the new digital challenges, and to finding new pedagogies to help colleagues "go where their students are" (the misguided vaguery demanded of us since we couldn't get them to come where we are) in constructive ways. Although my application was approved on all of the academic levels—chairman, dean, college president, provost—it got shot down at the top administrative level at the last minute. A reliable source reported to me that the bigwig who signed off on these had frowned at my project, and proclaimed, "I don't even know what this one is talking about!" and tossed the application aside with a red X on it. What I was talking about was "digital literacy." This person didn't have it, I didn't have enough of it, my colleagues for the most part didn't have enough of it; even our students didn't have it adequate to the academic and professional contexts. Why, as late as 2016, didn't everyone increasingly living online, have it?

Outrage and bitterness aside, I had some good outcomes of my FDL application process. First, I found out about a number of faculty, many of whom I had known as grad students at UT-Arlington in the '90s, who were developing new digital literacy pedagogies. I wish that I had the time and focus here to review my discoveries of all of their successes and publications. However, Douglas Eyman's 2015 *Digital Rhetoric: Theory, Method, Practice* proved another of those godsend texts reassuring me that I wasn't stupid, or misled, or mis-inclined to think about things that big administrators didn't know anything about. In fact, Eyman took a fellow wanderer's hand and guided her to realize several vital and enduring connections between the old and new worlds:

- That literacy has always been a function of humans working "digitally" with codes and has "always been a material, multi-media construct" (19);

- That what we call "rhetoric" as the art of persuasion has always been necessarily collaborative, and thus the new media "support and enable the transformation of the old rhetoric of persuasion into a new digital rhetoric that encourages self-expression, participation, and creative collaboration" (James Zappen qtd. in Eyman 27). This might be seen as, if not as an improvement, definitely an enhancement as contrasted with the "physical isolation of the printed work" (25), a state also noted by McLuhan.

- That digital literacy and rhetoric provide to educators exciting new pedagogic frontiers as he warns about " 'just [applying] traditional methods'. . . to analysis rather than considering whether qualities of new media or digital texts should be considered as new forms, perhaps requiring the development of new theory or method" (33).

As fond as I am of traditional methods of research and reading (yes, long and dense prose texts) and writing (even, or especially the five-paragraph essay), I have suspected that these methods run counter to a truly "student-centered" pedagogic frame nowadays. You might recall my boldly confessed scorn for this "student-centered" phrase as my question has always been: when have we NOT been student centered? Just because we give a lecture and require our students to take notes, must we be charged with being student uncentered? Anyway, buying into the concept that our students should at least in some contexts be in charge of the classroom, while hopefully we still teach them things, or at least "facilitate" while they teach themselves things, I will ask: how is forcing them to read and write entirely in the old print-literate modes being sensitive to where they live, nowadays? And with the exception of a few purist pioneers, most of us still teach this way because the required institutional/departmental SLO's (Student Learning Outcomes) demand it.

In 2015 Eyman notes and helpfully classifies the various paths of pedagogic wandering still underway in 2024: some choose to stick to traditional theories and practices for analyzing digital texts, some say these theories must be revised for "digital, networked communication," and some argue that altogether new theories and practices must be created (61). Instructors might classify themselves along these lines. At my advanced age and career stage, I might not embark on the third project, but I am still invested in the first two. As a longtime instructor of both domestic and international students, and along the lines of creating an equitable and inclusive classroom, I am especially impressed by how Eyman connects the need for new digital pedagogies to our new global connections, made possible by the internet and online education especially. Quoting Byron Hawke, Eyman reminds us that we must be sensitively aware of the "contemporary network space," as opposed to the old civic forums and the relative isolation of print literacy, and that "there are 'few rhetorical theories that adequately address the complexities of this new social space'"(81). Our students worldwide live in this network space, and we must be sure to realize that this new dominant text platform calls us to new, creative action as educators.

I realize that this new dominant text platform calls us to new, creative action as educators. As his title promises, Eyman offers many examples of "theory, method, practice" in this book. In fact, I have used several of his strategies in my classes, with fruitful results, including community college freshman English, ESL reading and writing courses, and special topics classes such as "Understanding Media" (also a basic college literacy course).

Never does he force educators to take a quantum leap into the new: a demand that is not only impossible but also undesirable. Echoing my thoughts above, quoting Sarah Arroyo, Eyman reminds us that "we are living in a time on the cusp where traditional literate practices are still highly valued." He very practically states:

> I have yet to encounter a digital rhetoric course whose products are only new media, but I believe that the perspectives gained by using the more familiar critical approaches in print literacy to reflect upon, analyze, and critique digital rhetoric production are a beneficial pedagogical practice and I hope that we do not shift to purely nonprint-media works in such courses as long as print literacy is still a dominant mechanism for knowledge production in our society. (115)

As an English instructor I am grateful to Dr. Eyman for not only supporting the impulse behind my failed FDL application, in the face of uber-Luddite (or just plain ignorant) rejection. I am grateful to him for providing to me foundation in both the theory and practice of teaching the new media; see a few of my more successful (enough) efforts just below. Finally, I am grateful to him for sharing his humanistic perspective, urging us to identify and innovate, as we are not merely falling to machine tyranny but learning to recognize "new patterns of thinking, rethinking familiar conceptualizations about both the self and human interaction, and re-envisioning attitudes and expectations towards reading, writing, and rhetoric, regardless of the physical presence of machines" (Arroyo, qtd. in Eyman 114). This approach allows us to leverage the successes of our past to help our students thrive in the future.

A few things I've tried

A whole course, no less...

Driven by curiosity and the need to work through so much negativity, the more I became obsessed with "mediacy" and my sense of wandering, the more I turned to my students for help. After all, the foundational reason I cared about all of this was for their sake. I could retire pretty soon, but they couldn't. Plus, I knew they were, or at least were rumored to be, already comfortable residents of that second world and word: the digital. If they were happy and productive, successful enough in this new world, who was I to complain?

Help came in 2013 when my college embarked on a three-year "Quality Enhancement Plan" (QEP) focused on critical thinking. I needed to incorporate the principal tenets of the QEP into my teaching practice. I began to scheme: it had become increasingly difficult to engage our Composition

II, Literary Analysis students with course content, including novels, short stories, plays, poems, essays, and more. Rounding up the usual suspects seemed to be the modus operandi behind reading list choices. I mean, I love Shakespeare, Emily Dickinson, Henry James, and Faulkner as much as anyone, but even I struggle to read these works. More and more of my students claimed that they "never read anything," freely confessing their preference for spending their time perusing online platforms.

We weren't prepared to move our course content entirely to the digital realm. Plus, Douglas Eyman and others have rejected this as not only impossible at this stage, given continued demands for print literacy throughout college and beyond, but also unreasonable for instructors shakily straddling the divide, who would not yet or ever know how to create and deliver such curriculum. So I decided to do the next best thing: offer my Comp II classes a theme that would attract students, and more importantly, one that would take us right into the heart of the matter. How has technology impacted our society and lives? How has this impact been registered in dystopian literature?

What follows describes a course that I developed and taught at the community college; Basing it in Composition II, I entitled it "American Dystopia" and used dystopian literature: fiction, poetry, plays, essays, other older forms as tools for my students as they excavated their life troubles. It became a very andragogic course, that is, one that not only allowed but also insisted that students align their life experiences with our concepts and materials and be major contributors to our course material. In fact, early on in a guided exercise, I had my class brainstorm and then create a list of "dystopian markers (DM)," general categories of evidence about societal deterioration and slippage into dystopia. Informed by their own life experience, my students came up with spot-on DM's, with guess what? Technology's overtaking of their lives, for the worse, took first place. Much like my World Lit students for Dante's nine circles of , my Dystopia students proved the techno-tyrant a common denominator threat embedded in all of the other DM's.

My spring 2016 class came up with the following DMs, and these pretty much represent what other semesters came up with; students derived these from our readings and also their sense of their own greatest challenges. They identified the markers listed below, and I have provided the results of their considering the technology link among all of them.

Culture of fear	Constant plug-in to saturation of bad news
	Fearmongering and bullying in social media
Individual vs. State	Surveillance
Biology vs. machine	Artificial intelligence
Reality vs. illusion	Fake News
"Amusing Ourselves to Death" (Postman)	Life consumed, frivolously and harm fully, on screens

Their identification of the dominant technology threat was both gratifying and distressing. I had wanted to dismiss my paranoia as inevitable old fogey-ism; I had hoped my students could be canny digital citizens in confident control of their experience. Instead, both digital immigrants and natives faced the six-headed dystopian beast above; and this would give us such a wonderful "student-centered" class where instructor and students alternated as Virgil and Dante, wandering and critically thinking through the new Inferno and Purgatorio. I was not generationally alone in navigating the Divide, struggling in the dark forest of confusion and even despair over what the Technopolists had in store for us.

But back to the course itself. We started out with a survey of classic utopias, from Plato to Thomas More to Karl Marx. This would give us a sense of how utopia is always just the other side of the coin; in fact, it is the desire and quest to create utopias that prove mainly responsible for dystopias, a fact nowhere more evident than in our current worship of information technology. Looking back to Milton, a mythic way to see this is Satan's promise to pervert to evil whatever God gives His children for their good. From there, we moved to the dystopian Big Daddy, George Orwell and *1984*. You'd have to have lived in a remote cave, or at least stayed off social media, not to recognize the contemporary relevance of a story about screens in every room for Big Brother to dominate, control, and oppress us under the guise of supporting, teaching, and entertaining us. Next, we did units on dystopian fiction, film, and media. My favorite text among these was *Black Mirror*; we watched the episodes "Fifteen Million Merits" and "Nosedive." These episodes revealed the horror potential of virtual life, smartphone addiction, media-driven social credit scores, and other examples of how the embraced present can hold the quickly germinating seeds of a dystopian future.

Finally, our unit on scholarly dystopia introduced my charges to some of my heroes, principally Neil Postman (*Amusing Ourselves to Death* and *Technopoly*), Mark Bauerlein (*The Dumbest Generation*), Sherry Turkle (*Alone Together*) and David Skrbina (*The Metaphysics of Technology*). These are very challenging writers and texts, and my colleagues thought me way too ambitious and, I believe, misguided and even insane to assign these to my freshmen. My students proved them wrong, and I got some of the best papers of my career from our final writing assignment: to close-analyze a passage from one of these writers.

I am the most proud of their efforts on our dystopia capstone assignment, described below:

> Each student will focus on one subtopic area of utopian/dystopian culture and develop a coherent project tying together definition and development of issues, media coverage, literary connections and pop-culture manifestations of your focus topic. Your project will conclude with a creative and critical-thinking-driven solution to the dystopic focus. Your Course Project is in essay format but can include visuals, film, music, art, hyperlinks and other digital support. Our course final exam is your presentation of the project, with your choice of format: PowerPoint, Prezi, YouTube, photographic essay, posters, anything else creative.

I no longer have access to most of their specific titles, but I recall their topic choices with a grateful heart and mind. Their topics included dystopian angles on the military and warfare, environment, the food industry, health care, rape culture, bullying, and of course, technology. We presented these in a small auditorium and invited the campus; attendance was good. We had a Costco cake inscribed with "Taste the Dystopia." I am always proud of my students, but this day, my cup surely ranneth over. I figure that if you can squeeze this much joy out of dystopia, there is hope. Just work with your students and trust them to help you find the joy and the hope, the adventure, even through the dark forest.

Metacognitive, at least

I have never meant to suggest anywhere that a lot of good work in new digital literacies hasn't been done in higher academics; there is ample evidence to the contrary, for example with one powerful 2004 article. It's just that I myself wasn't doing it or doing or learning enough of it. The fact that I have taught, in the past three decades, in four different institutions' English departments, has informed me that in the mainstream, this work is still not emphasized as a primary call to English instructors and "content experts." In the last couple of decades, I began to be troubled by this sense of disconnection between my traditional pedagogy and practice and the needs and habits of my students. It wasn't so much about what they needed as what they didn't seem to need: classwork and assignments based in the individual, detached, linear, slow, long, progressive modes of print literacy. Either they wouldn't, or they couldn't; mostly, they just didn't. More and more of my students would fail to submit assignments. Once, when asking them to critically evaluate the argument of a long article, I got this submission, and this alone: "tl;dr." Disappointed and intrigued, I approached the student. "Too long, didn't read," he translated. But, but, but I stumbled, you can't do that. My need to give him the zero was eclipsed by my need to understand his motivation here; he was a bright, apparently intelligent and avid class participator. Why wouldn't he do my assignment?

The above-referenced 2004 article is "Teaching Digital Rhetoric: Community, Critical Engagement, and Application," published by DigiRhet. org and reporting from Digital Rhetoric, a course taught in the Michigan State University's Professional Writing Program in Fall 2004. This article is a rich repository of theory and practice for new digital literacies, it is still very much worth attentive and respectful reading. I did not come across it until I prepared my ill-fated FDL proposal around 2016; if I had found it sooner, I surely would have started altering my own theory and practice in its intelligent and innovative directions. You see, at this point, I was only about three years before official retirement age. My FDL on digital literacy I had intended to launch a post-retirement redirection for me, as a student and then scholar-practitioner of digital literacy in some future venue, likely adjunct but who cared? How exciting, to find a new frontier three-plus decades into one's career. However, not receiving the FDL, being called to retire from my full-time teaching job and return to my home state to care for a parent, and other changes put a brake on my frontier trajectory. When I did get a new job, it was teaching the English language to international students, also a career-long interest. Although in this capacity I have gotten to teach certificate classes like "English for Social Media," I have had neither the platform nor focused learning opportunities to develop adequately my digital literacy chops for composition classes.

Occasionally I will meet a student who says something like, "I actually love English but I'm going into IT (Information Technology), so I can earn a living." I jump to say, "why don't you combine both?" As the DigiRhet authors argue, becoming digitally literate, in service of our students' needs, is the most important call to action for educators today. Our digital natives' prowess does not necessarily reach into their academic and professional lives. It is our job to help them fill this need, as:

> [E]ach student needs to understand how their professional lives will be affected by issues of digital rhetoric, as well as how a better understanding of digital rhetoric and digital technologies will benefit them in their postgraduation careers...How do we answer Hawisher and Selfe's call for new pedagogies that facilitate our students' "messy transition" to a multimodal culture while still acknowledging their current individual, culturally situated literacies [that is, READING]? We posit that we do so by returning to our students' needs in the digital writing classroom — that is, the need for community, the need for critical engagement, and the need for practical application. (248)

This language reminds me of characteristics of today's students. They are more tolerant, inclusive and companionate in the classroom. They like to work together, in pairs or small groups, countering my own distaste for group work. They need to know why they should do what they are asked to do, how this will specifically benefit them, a critical move that my generation would never have thought to make. According to DigiRhet, fulfilling these needs is one of the more exciting promises of digital literacy as digital texts, platforms and operations require "community," collaboration and moving critically and analytically in multiple goal-oriented directions.

Fortunately for this old print-literate instructor, the call to action, at least the foundational 2004 one, seems familiar. The so-called digital-native immigrant to true digital literacy must start somewhere.

Assignments that address critical engagement should encourage students to critique the influence of technology on their communication practices, identity, and bodies. These activities should spotlight the ways in which we negotiate identity (both individual and community), literacy, power, and agency within computer-mediated environments. Students must be called to examine and reexamine their relationships with the technologies they employ regularly. Critical engagement assignments should also ask students to examine the societal and/or cultural constructs influenced by technology (DigiRhet 249).

This breakdown of how to fulfill community/critical engagement/application struck me as necessarily metacognitive, a hot topic in teaching and learning in the twenty-teens and still today. Finally, this vision, for me as a new learner, demanded a student-centered and andragogic classroom; my students reported being on so many internet and social media platforms of which I had never even heard. I finally joined Facebook in 2013 when three students stormed into my office, pulled me out of my desk seat, and occupied my computer, asking me different personal questions about myself. Thinking they needed this for some kind of application, I answered their questions. Then, the disrupter banging on my keyboard stood up and announced, "Dr. Sapp, you finally have a Facebook page." "Take it down!" I screamed. "It's unprofessional not to have a social media presence," they countered. Oh, well, OK...I couldn't help but agree even if I didn't like it. As Facebook would remain my only contact with cyber-society, I had to rely on them to teach me the new ways.

Read on to learn about some of the assignments I learned from DigiRhet and successfully tried out in my Composition classes. More metacognitive than technical—and this is at least a temporary necessity for the immigrant instructor—these assignments flipped my classroom as students taught me about the technical, communal, critical, and applied dimensions of their digital lives.

Evolving Brains and Classrooms

Gary Small and Gigi Vorgan, in "Your Brain Is Evolving Right Now," excerpted from iBrain, define yet another important divide or "gap" to consider when we older educators think about our troubles connecting with our classes the way we once could:

> Today's young people in their teens and twenties, who have been dubbed Digital Natives, have never known a world without computers, twenty-four-hour TV news, Internet, and cell phones—with their video, music, cameras and text messaging . . . The neural networks in the brains of these Digital Natives differ dramatically from those of the Digital Immigrants: people—including all baby boomers—who came to the digital/computer age as adults but whose brain wiring was laid down during a time when direct social interaction was the norm . . . . As a consequence of this overwhelming and early high-tech stimulation of the Digital Native's brain, we are witnessing the beginning of a deeply divided brain gap between younger and older minds—in just one generation . . . Individuals of the older generation face a world in which their brains must adapt to high technology or they'll be left behind—politically, socially, and economically. (78–9)

Here Small and Vorgan summarize a possible source of the older educator's wandering fog: the difference between the print-literate brain (they pin it on "direct social interaction," also a factor) and the digitally wired brain. In my experience, even my younger colleagues have struggled to "meet our students where they are," that popular rallying cry, due to students' unwillingness if not inability to focus and sustain attention to our primarily print-literate-based assignments, for example novels, scholarly articles and essays. The final paper assignment gradually became a nightmare beyond rational tolerance due to late or no submission, plagiarism, and inability to sustain a line of argument. Multiply this times maybe a hundred submissions, and something had to change. For the sake of their future coursework and professional lives transacted in a still largely print-literature methodology (in many if not most fields), we had to insist on some rigor in traditional skill acquisition. However, we increasingly struggled against an anti-print-literacy tide identified by such as Nicholas Carr:

> Mark Federman, an education researcher at the University of Toronto, argued that literacy, as we've traditionally understood it, 'is now nothing but a quaint notion . . . no longer the structuring force of society.' The time has come, he said for teachers and students alike to abandon the 'linear, hierarchical' world of the book and enter the Web's 'world of ubiquitous connectivity and pervasive proximity'— a world in which 'the greatest skill' involves 'discovering emergent meaning among contexts that are continually in flux' . . . Our old literary habits 'were just a side-effect of living in an environment of impoverished access.' (111–112)

To put things more familiarly, my own old print brain proved so lame that I had no idea how to create assignments that would tap-in to a putative universe (Library of Babel?) of enriched access. It was late in my career, and I was pretty burnt out, though still deeply invested in my students' welfare. Plus, as Small and Vorgan insist, we have no choice in the matter: we must learn the digitally rewired ways or kiss our careers goodbye. When I stumbled across the DigiRhet.org publication, I felt my print fog lift just enough to see some digital light. And that light took the form of the flipped classroom + metacognition. I would let my students play all they wanted to on the internet; but they'd have to work for that privilege, at least in part using print-literate platforms, to pass my ENG 101 class. Medium and message could work together in mutually informative ways.

This turned out to be a great meeting between print and digital minds. Based on DigiRhet models, I created three assignments that we used as a capstone Comp I assignment. Since these put my students through all the traditional critical-analysis paces, and they could hang out on the internet while pacing, excellent work got done.

1. Digital Grammar—Put a "digital spin" on standard sentence grammar and style by emphasizing the structure, length, clarity, style, and rhetoric desirable in print-literate writing and comparing these to social media (SM) writing features; and teach strategies

for more powerful and effective communication both print and online. For our text here, we used not only SM postings but also and especially the comments, which we analyzed for the above-listed features and as a bonus, had a lot of laughs. I gave them charts to fill for these elements, and the students put their knowledge of new SM composition practices to the test. We included a lesson on code-switching defined as print-to-digital.

2. Cyber Turkey. Get your students to go "cold turkey" for 24 hours on their smartphones. Have them keep a journal of their feelings, experiences, challenges and reliefs felt during this eternal stretch. Even if they made it only one hour, they could complete the assignment by answering bail-out questions.

3. Cyber Pie (Chart, that is). Have your students track their phone/internet usage for 24 hours. Have them take detailed notes on their experiences. Then, have them create a pie chart or other data chart showing their usage categories: social, shopping, school, surfing, music, and more. Finally, have them analyze their usage and comment on its effect on their personal, work and academic life. (Thanks to colleague and friend John T. Martin for this one.)

4. Social-Media Circus. Have your students come up with all of the "social media" examples they can, and then have them self-divide into small groups according to their interests. Have each group do research on its chosen medium, including the following information:
   - History—when, where and how was it launched?
   - People behind it—who started it, how and why?
   - How it works—both practical and aesthetic elements
   - Sampling and analysis of its discourse—from quotes taken from the medium. How does this medium make meaning? What kinds of structures and styles does it favor?
   - Advantages and disadvantages of the medium: how has it affected my own life?
   - Multi-Media Presentation—From their research, each group will present a poster, Power Point, Prezi, YouYube, any combination thereof or other creative way to teach the class all about that particular social medium.

As early as 1969, Neil Postman reliably summarized the highest wisdom for today's educator: "Clearly, there is no more important function for education to fulfill than that of helping us to recognize the world we actually live in and, simultaneously, of helping us to master concepts that will increase our ability to cope with it. This is the essential criterion for judging the relevance of all education" (*Teaching* 212). And this applies to both sides of the podium: instructors must recognize and include the digital world our students and all of us actually live in most of the time while sharing with them concepts that will increase their ability to cope with the changes brought about by the new media to their human(istic) lives and their brain wiring. For as a literature search of the past twenty years will inform you—it's no picnic on either side of the divide.

If you are a young instructor (or an older one who's had no issue with all of this), in any case you have kept on reading, for which I thank you. I also advise you to jump right into writing new pedagogy for the digital age. For as Postman also has warned, "It obviously makes no sense in trying to build a vehicle for a mission in space to use the blueprints, materials, and terminology appropriate to building a steamboat . . . We have new languages to learn if we don't want to talk ourselves to death" (*Teaching* 169). There is work to do, colleagues, so let's get on it.

CHAPTER 9: IS REALITY ON MY SIDE? A CONCLUSION TO A START

> First follow NATURE, and your judgment frame
> By her just standard, which is still the same:
> Unerring Nature, still divinely bright,
> One clear, unchang'd, and universal light...
>
> —Alexander Pope, Essay on Criticism

> And technology proceeds apace.
>
> —David Skrbina

Let us first take a short trip on the Wayback Machine, back to 1968 and a text, a movie that had us all enthralled, terrified, wondering. I refer of course to Stanley Kubrick's *2001: A Space Odyssey*. I watched it again last night and recalled how many hours we spent as teens, speculating about that monolith: what was it? What was its purpose? Having devoured every episode of *Black Mirror* at least three times, the answer now seems obvious to me, that Kubrick was a prophet a la McLuhan (who had put out his *Understanding Media* in 1964), that the monolith was indeed an IPhone. This is a connection that many have made since the phone's arrival among us apes. One reviewer (Collative Learning) more generically points to Kubrick's likely self-referential symbolism: the monolith as screen. I like this latter because it aligns with my own erasure of a clear distinction between digital "natives" and "immigrants": born in 1953, I myself never had a moment without a screen at the center of my consciousness (i.e. my parents' black-and-white in our living room seventy years ago). Most of us alive today are, at least and in some form, screen natives.

When the information industry goes entirely to machines, they can tell us anything they want. That's so scary; I'd rather trust a human, warts, logical fallacies, and all, thank you. So I dared to pick a little on Sir Ken, young Logan, and entrepreneur Eddy; however, I dread a world where no one would have the passion and wherewithal to present their original ideas and experiences to us and where we'd feel no need to pick at because we have no idea who or what we're picking at or why we'd even need to. One ironic remedy remains: everyone forgets that when the money stops, the plug is pulled. Having put all of our information and knowledge eggs into that cold electronic basket—what happens when the money's gone? We are forced to recall our human personal agency. Forced back to quill and scroll, I guess, to writing everything with pencil and paper in the classroom. I've seen my students' handwriting, and that alone might force me to pray that someone always pays the bill.

They have beaten us.

I refer here not to students who refuse to get off their phones or stop plagiarizing from the internet. I do not mean the social media that have been eating our children's brains, driving them to depression, suicide and violence. I do not even mean ChatGPT, with its plagiarism-on-steroids as our current harbinger of doom, defeat and despair on the academic front and possibly human as well.

The culprit who has beaten us is capitalism and the takeover of education by the business model.

It is the business model that drives the internet. Ursula LeGuin has opined, "We live in capitalism. Its power seems inescapable. So did the divine right of kings. Any human power can be resisted and changed by human beings" (speech, National Book Awards 2014). She believed that art, especially writing, can resist and change the damage inflicted by profiteering.

I would love to embrace LeGuin's optimism as I have for a half-century dedicated my educator's humanist-liberal arts life and work to her claim. But I tend to align with Oliver Sacks, who a few years later lamented: "But it may not be enough to create, to contribute, to have influenced others if one feels, as I do now, that the very culture in which one was nourished, and to which one has given one's best in return, is itself threatened." This is the sense, the anxiety, the wandering through the dark forest between two worlds. My humanist intention and craft cannot save the world if the world is no longer able to recognize and understand the ways of either my intention or craft. Jonathan Haidt, in his well-titled *Atlantic* article "After Babel: How Social Media Dissolved the Mortar of Society and Made America

Stupid," breaks down the problem: "...by rewiring everything in a head-long rush for growth—with a naïve conception of human psychology, little understanding of the intricacy of institutions, and no concern for external costs imposed on society—Facebook, Twitter, YouTube, and a few other large platforms unwittingly dissolved the mortar of trust, belief in institutions, and shared stories that had held a large and diverse secular democracy together." The culture in which I was nourished was the print literate paradigm, the one in which shared personal stories are valuable and a primary goal; the one that threatens to destroy my culture is the digital literate, where even our stories might end up impersonal, algorithmic, fragmented, "multitasked," inhuman and ultimately inhumane.

Yesterday I had a phone call from a colleague at my former employment. He was almost breathless telling me about the physical changes being made on our campus. All instructors' private offices are to be removed; faculty and students will meet now in public spaces called "sticky," "neighborhood," "the balcony," and more ill-assigned metaphors. As I myself did, most of my colleagues had personal libraries in their small private offices. No more of these. I had a coffee maker, pretty porcelain cups, and a drawer full of cookies and chocolate for my visiting students. Some told me that it was the first time anyone had ever made coffee for them. My visiting students and I sat in cozy, book-lined privacy drinking coffee and talking about their concerns. No one else could see or hear us. Now, the instructors will sit at long tables with their visiting students sitting across from them practically elbow-to-elbow with the instructor and student seated on either side of each.

Who can think this is a good idea? This kills any privacy or sense of personal connection between instructor and student, not to mention quiet, reflective conversation. And motivation behind this is the hive mind, born of and borne by the internet: the drive to connection, collaboration, and "engagement" across multiple horizons in the scattershot goals and strategies of multitasking. This is the remaining physical environment of the University of Everywhere. My colleague told me that in the glossy publication distributed about this remodeling, there is actual language about driving out the old guard, reducing the expensive ranks of older, tenured faculty. *Cui bono?* You see how the true goal here is economic: reducing costs. Older, established faculty will not work under these conditions if they have the option to retire or do something else. Even if not going completely virtual and abandoning brick and mortar altogether, the college aims to operate mostly with adjunct faculty used to the digital economy, much like the online diploma mills with their vast stables of low-paid human grading machines.

I do not want to deal with ChatGPT; I do not want to sit in an open-spaced hive to greet my students, in a panopticon prison designed not first even to spy on us, which is at least interesting from the dystopian perspective, but rather to cut costs at the institution after spending millions to effect the necessary building remodeling. I do not want to continue to have to learn new time-consuming and bamboozling new technologies, however interesting and fun these might be (not to mention efficient), to teach English language and literature. **I do not want to spend the rest of my precious life, or at least career, "grading" the output of a bot.** I must, however, continue to teach because I love being with students and learning alongside them and maybe bringing to that learning collaboration some old analytic and critical tools (not to mention spiritual), to help us all continue to feel some sense of human value and agency as technology takes over more and more of our efforts and lives. Maybe I can even get them to slow down and think about things, especially those that are trying to harm them, to lure them away from their humanity, to rob them of their own stories that are their most powerful weapon against dehumanization.

A beginning to an end

In his aptly titled *Stolen Focus*, Johann Hari warns all of us tech-dependent and addicted, "...you may even begin 'decohering.' This is when you stop making sense to yourself because you don't have the mental space to create a story about who you are. You become obsessed with petty goals or dependent on simplistic signals from the outside world like retweets. You lose yourself in a cascade of distractions. You can only find your starlight and your daylight if you have sustained periods of reflection, mind-wandering, and deep thought. Our attention crisis is depriving us of all three of these forms of focus. We are losing our light" (267).

Last summer, I had decohering smack me in the face. I was teaching the summer English college-prep camp for advanced high-school students. I must first say that my students were angels, and the three-week camp was overall successful, fun, and helpful for them. We especially enjoyed our flipped class, where these students formally introduced me to the demon bot and its seductive ways. But one small but overwhelming example of decohering tends to dominate my memory of our experience together.

Our lesson was, anachronistically, "the application essay." I say anachronistically because, to my current knowledge, many universities are eliminating this requirement, presumably due to the likelihood that too many submissions are not original. Writing students' application essays has been a booming business in the academic gig economy. These plagiarist sites, staffed by humans, are now doomed by the bot that can crank out essays much, much faster and more efficiently. Live by the sword, die by the sword.

Anyway, we were using the Common Application's six prompts, all calling for writers to draw from their personal experiences, feelings, judgments, hopes, dreams, etc. Thinking this was pretty straightforward, I set my class to drafting; thirty minutes later, only two of the fifteen had managed to start. "I don't understand what it is you want us to do"—possibly the most annoying language string possible for the instructor who has done everything but plant a chip in her students' brains to guide them through the assignment process. But annoyance immediately sublimates into helpfulness, so I said, "Just pick a topic and tell your story. Tell a story that happened to you about this. Start by free-writing your story; jot down the who-what-where-when-how-why details of it." Feeling satisfied that this would do the trick, I returned to my seat and waited.

Fifteen minutes pass, and keyboards are clicking. Good! I get up to wander around and see how they are getting started. And what do I see but students frantically googling the terms topic-free-writing-jot-where-when-how-why and even, goddess save us, story. Not a one of them was actually writing their story; they apparently did not trust their instructor enough with her English professor's definition of the word "story." They had to google it before they could begin to understand what this is. You don't have the mental space to create a story of who you are. You have become, by the tender age of 16, dependent on simplistic signals from the outside world like retweets—and certainly google, and now AI. When our students don't even know the meaning of "story," much less their own version of one, "they" have beaten us.

Enlightenment

Dante Alighieri lost his light when his love, Beatrice, died young, leaving him in catastrophic grief and unshielded against the political turmoil and general human treachery of his time, as in all time. He lost his own story. With the poet Virgil coming to his rescue as he wandered through the dark forest, Dante literally went through hell, worked through Purgatory, and eventually, with the guidance of angel Beatrice, came to the light, which was God, into which he could not stare directly, like one can into a screen. What is our light today? Johann Hari suggests that this light is found within us and requires time, silence, and aloneness to achieve: precisely the three needs from which the internet distracts us, if not destroys the capability.

The internet has reprogrammed us for false connections, collaborations, contributions. Remember that you cannot sit silently in a class or small group, reflecting on your own thoughts in relation to the presented lesson material; you must Pez-dispense verbal bytes and earn your points for the data machine, to prove that Student Learning Outcomes have been achieved and aligned with the inevitable institutional rubric, another increasingly required data-processing tool in higher ed these days.

It is fitting to include here a final nod to adolescent psychologist Jean Twenge, author of *IGen: Why Today's Super-Connected Kids Are Growing Up Less Rebellious, More Tolerant, Less Happy and Completely Unprepared for Adulthood—and What That Means for the Rest of Us*. In a 2024 CNN interview, Dr. Twenge described the recent exponential rise in teen anxiety and depression, suicide, and violence to themselves and others. She observes, "We tried to blame this on the pandemic," but then traces its origins to around 2010, the time the smartphone reached its electronic tentacles back into early adolescence and even late childhood, when having a phone became de rigueur for tween social belonging and interaction.

Like many other critiques of phones and social media, starting with William Powers' *Hamlet's Blackberry* (2010) to Nicholas Carr's *The Shallows* (2020) and more recently, Johan Hari, Jonathan Haidt, and a lot of others, Twenge's *IGen* takes on the question: can we fix this? Answers abound, such as personal discipline to put the device down, parental interference, tech producers installing more protective software, etc. Some colleges now in 2023 are even taking the ridiculously useless step of "banning ChatGPT on their campus." Well, plagiarism has always been banned on campuses, but such bans are worth precisely their amount of wasted cyber-ink in student online handbooks. Many K-12 schools are valiantly working to stop cell-phone usage during school classroom hours.

The truth is, though, that there isn't much we can do. The technology is too seductive, available, saturated, entertaining, and informative for us to self-regulate. (My high school students admit to spending eight hours and more, after school, online on social media and video games. "When do you sleep?" "We don't, much.") As Hari astutely suggests, self-regulation is a sort of red herring in questions of mitigating technology's adverse effects. It is too profitable for tech companies to limit its applications. As they say, you can't force the genie back into the bottle. In *The Metaphysics of Technology*, David Skrbina claims that what we live through, always, is technology asserting its dominance over us as it is the very energy fabric of the universe. We are just one component, one cog of it. Perhaps we know we are a failed experiment and are using technology to destroy ourselves, so something better can evolve. Some enthusiasts, rejecting Dr. Skrbina's apocalyptic tone, argue that this is a good thing: why should we believe that we are the ontological telos of the universe? Surely it can and will do better! So maybe this next world, liberated from the messy inconvenience of the human physical body, will be a better one. Until, that is, something better gets itself created by and gets to work destroying the technology prior to it, to create its new dominance. Notice I say "dominance" instead of "progress." Progress is a manmade, utopian concept. The universe is a raw power struggle, and yes, literally. Maybe I should contact ChatGPT and get its opinion on all this. After all, why trust my human paranoia and fallibility when we can go to the source? Why listen to limited, print-wired me whining about my restricted mortal path through time and (cyber)space when we can consult an AI capable of aggregating vast amounts and kinds of data, the infinite fruits of the hive mind, the Library of Babel? What does Chat think of itself and its purpose in the universe? What if I have finally caved and used it to write this paragraph? Hey, I'm starting to like this movie! Dystopian or apocalyptic? Time will tell.

Cultivate your garden

I am tired and need to quit.

I wish I felt this way about teaching, but I don't, so I'll hang in there. I wrote this book to reach out to all of you who are or who have been teachers—present, past, and future—students, families of these, lifelong learners, both willing and forced consumers of technology; who are exhausted, confused, anxious, depressed, defeated; who are wandering in confusion, doubt, and even despair through what is happening these days. I am surely no Virgil, but I've had some experiences and have some ideas. I hope I have kept you company and given you hope, at least that there are others out there feeling the way you do. I'm sure I have displeased or triggered some of you, especially in the TED Talk chapter. I mean, who in their right mind would pick on TED Talks, not to mention talented teenagers presenting them, not to mention my own logically fallacious argument there based on just three samples.

I mean, I need to quit writing now. The process has proven exhilarating and exhausting, with every day bringing a new point of interest, event, threat, and challenge to the experience of wandering between these worlds and words: print and digital, human and machine. This will never end. Glued to the array of sources on my devices, my attention oscillates among tech threats, fake news, political circuses, hate crimes, and mass shootings; how long can one cope with this?

What can we do to make it all better? Probably not put down our phones or go off the grid. These are not good solutions and likely can't happen, for reasons both bad and good. Technology is not a problem with a solution: it is the vehicle of a paradigm shift. We must ride it out and cross it, this divide between the comfortable old and the challenging new, like it or not.

I tell my students to put their phones down long enough to do some yoga and grow a garden. These are the only two pastimes of my life that have simmered down my anxiety to an almost tolerable level. I get down on the classroom floor and attempt the lotus position or anything close to it, still impossible after forty-some years of practice: "But I'm still here doing the work," I assure them. The same is true in my classroom. Don't pass it off to alien bots; show up and do the work yourself, get knowledgeable and strong. You will like the way this feels, energizing as opposed to enervating. Many of my students join me and pop right into full lotus, and these aren't necessarily the young ones. The happiest people I know are the ones who show up to try and who work hard and love their work.

Move your body in interesting and helpful ways outside or on sports fields and hiking trails, in dance and yoga classes. Stop sexting and have sex. Spend as much time as you can in nature, maybe even trying to grow and eat some stuff out of it. Now I will close with one more of my lesson plans and wait for it—it's a TED Talk. I know, I know...but this one isn't grounded in logical fallacies and rhetorical stunts, trying to cram an iconoclasm or at least a mind-blowing "disruption" into twelve minutes. Ron Finley takes just 10.46 minutes for his "A Guerrilla Gardener in South Central L.A." (2013), and his proposal is practical and doable by many if not most of us. Mr. Finley has walked the walk, so I am willing to hear him talk the Talk. A longtime community member himself, he describes his successful efforts to start converting a community riddled with poverty, crime, and disease into a self-determining gardening community where residents can eat more fresh produce that they themselves have produced, become healthier in body and mind as a result, and thus start to improve all parts of life. He includes photos before and after from his community: from wheelchair kiosks and dialysis centers (O.K., a couple of rhetorical stunts) to Edenic gardens, planted in vacant lots, along streets, and on medians, offering this repletion to all takers, for free.

My students can't help but fall in vegetable love with Ron, as I have done; however, they can be sharp skeptics and don't let him get away free. "Yeah, just ask my neighbors to beat their guns into plowshares and see how far that gets you." I understand their concern; Finley's vision has its utopic aura as well. But others around the nation have started their own projects, including

New Haven, CT, that literally beat guns into gardening tools after getting some citizens to exchange the former for compensation. Who doesn't love gardening? Nothing short of mankind's first story features it prominently, and if our first parent had just stuck to gardening instead of reaching for the fatal knowledge, extended persuasively by guess who, we might have avoided much unpleasantness, including that covered in this book.

I love discussing with and recommending gardening and yoga to my students because these cannot be done on screens. I know there are yoga classes online, but most everyone prefers the physical class environment for the best experience. At any rate, you must do yoga with your own physical body, and you are even invited to love your body and feel gratitude for its potential within the practice. As for the garden, none of that can be done on screens. Plus, if you try to do yoga or garden while holding a phone, it will get sweaty and grimy, although many insist on trying. There's no one more hated in yoga class than that inevitable addict who clutches the phone throughout practice, and sounds issuing from it in the midst of savasana could motivate violence, even among the most zenned-out. We hate these yoga-class phone offenders even more than the loud grunters. And if in the garden you insist, even if absent-mindedly wielding a shovel, on staying bent over your phone, "staring at your own foul and lazy mist" while out in nature, "in the sweet air made gladsome by the sun," you're going to hell, you unrepentant.

Personally, I like the advice the wine goddess Siduri gives to Gilgamesh, who is trying to defeat mortality: the one enemy, along with technology, equally impossible to defeat. She tells him to eat, drink, make love, and make merry, to enjoy his days and love his children.

Love our children. Be their responsible human mentor. And always keep learning about, with and for them. Me, quit?

Namaste.

Bibliography

Abrams, Amanda. "An Education in Scrolling." *Indy Week*, September 4, 2024, 4-5.

Alin, Pauli (2020). "Detecting and prosecuting contract cheating with evidence—a 'Doping Test' approach, International Journal for Educational Integrity." Vol.16, Number 7, 2020, 2-13.

Aschoff, Nicole. *The Smartphone Society: Technology, Power, and Resistance in the New Gilded Age*. Beacon Press, Boston, 2020.

Audry, Rebecca and Phillip Newton. *Higher Education*. Dordrecht, Vol. 78, Iss. 4, Sep 2019.

Baron, Naomi S.. *Always On: Language in an Online and Mobile World*. Oxford University Press, 2008.

Bauerlein, Mark. *The Digital Divide: Arguments for and Against Facebook, Google, Texting, and the Age of Social Networking*. Jeremy P. Tarcher/Penguin, 2011.

_____. *The Dumbest Generation: How the Digital Age Stupefies Young Americans and Jeopardizes Our Future (Or, Don't Trust Anyone Under 30)*. Jeremy P. Tarcher/Penguin, 2019.

Benjamin, Walter. *The Work of Art in the Age of Mechanical Reproduction*. Classic Books of America, 1935.

Benedikt, Michael. "Cityspace, Cyberspace and Spatiology of Information." *Journal of Virtual Worlds Research*, Vol. 1., No. 1, July 2008.

Berman, Morris. *The Twilight of American Culture*. W.W. Norton & Company, 2000.

Bridle, James. *New Dark Age: Technology and the End of the Future*. Verso, 2018.

Carey, Kevin. *The End of College: Creating the Future of Learning and the University of Everywhere*. Riverhead Books 2016.

Carr, Nicholas. *The Shallows: What the Internet is Doing to Our Brains*. W.W. Norton & Co., 2010.

Deresiewicz, W . "The End of Solitude." *The Chronicle of Higher Education*, January 20, 2009.

DigiRhet.org. "Teaching Digital Rhetoric: Community, Critical Engagement, and Application." *Pedagogy*, Duke University Press, Vol. 6, Iss. 2, Spring 2006.

Ellis, Cath, et. al." The Infernal business of contract cheating: understanding the business processes and models of academic custom writing sites." *International Journal for Educational Integrity*, Heidelberg, Vol. 14, Iss. 1, Dec 2018.

Ellul, Jacques. *The Technological Bluff*. Wm. B. Eerdmans Publishing Co., 1990

Emergent Tech. "27 Words and phrases that make it obvious you used ChatGPT," July 09, 2024 03:46 PM GST.

Eyman, Douglas. *Digital Rhetoric*. University of Michigan Press, 2015.

Finley, Ron. *A Guerrilla Gardener in South Central L.A.* TEDTalks, 2013.

Ginsberg, Benjamin. *The Fall of the Faculty: The Rise of the All-Administrative University and Why It Matters*. Oxford University Press, 2011.

Giroux, Henry A. Truthout. "The Specter of Authoritarianism and the Future of the Left," Interview by CJ Polychroniou, *Truthout*, June 8, 2014.

Gitlin, Todd. *Media Unlimited: How the Torrent of Images and Sounds Overwhelms Our Lives*. Henry Holt and Company, 2002.

Haidt, Jonathan. "After Babel: How Social Media Dissolved the Mortar of Society and Made America Stupid." *The Atlantic*, May 2022.

____ *The Anxious Generation: How the Great Rewiring of Childhood is Causing an Epidemic of Mental Illness*. Penguin Press, 2024.

Hari, Johann. *Stolen Focus: Why You Can't Pay Attention and How To Think Deeply Again*. Crown, 2022.

Heidegger, M. *The Question Concerning Technology and Other Essays*. Harper Torchbooks, 1982.

Hume, David. *A Treatise of Human Nature*. 1739.

Hussin, Habsah and Ismael Maimunah. "Plagiarism: More than Meets the Eye." *Advances in Language and Literary Studies*, Vol.4, No. 2, July 2013.

Huxley, Aldous. *Brave New World*. 1932.

Illich, Ivan. *Tools for Conviviality*. Marian Boyers Publishers, 2021.

Indick, William. *The Digital God: How Technology Will Reshape Spirituality*. McFarland & Company, Inc., 2015.

Jameson, Fredric. *Postmodernism, or the Cultural Logic of Late Capitalism*. Duke University Press, 1991.

Joy, Bill. "Why the Future Doesn't Need Us." *Wired*, Issue 8, April 2000.

Kelly, Kevin. *What Technology Wants*. TEDxSF, 2010.

Kirp, David. L. "Teaching is Not a Business." *New York Times Sunday Review*, August 14, 2014..

Kirsch, Adam. :Technology is Taking Over English Departments: The false promise of the digital humanities." *The New Republic*, May 2, 2014.

Lancaster, Thomas and Corinne Hersey. "The Online Industry of Paper Mills Contract Cheating Services and Auction Sites." Clute Institute International Education, London, June 2015.

LaPlante, Logan. "Hackschooling Makes Me Happy". TEDEx University of Nevada, Feb. 13 2013.

McCullough, Gretchen. *Because Internet: Understanding the New Rules of Language*. Riverhead Books, 2019.

McLuhan, Marshall. *Understanding Media: The Extensions of Man*. MIT edition, 1994.

_____. "Interview with *Playboy* magazine." *Playboy*, Vol. 16, No. 3, 1969, 53-74.

McMurtrie, Beth and Beckie Supiano. *Chronicle of Higher Education-Brave New World*. June 13, 2023.

O'Neil, Megan. "Confronting the Myth of the Digital Native." *The Chronicle of Higher Education*, May 2 2013.

Pecorari, Diane and Bojana Petric. "Plagiarism in Second-Language Writing." *Language Teaching*: Cambridge, Vol. 47, Iss. 3, July 2014, 269-302.

Petcoff, Omonpee W. *Exploring Emoji as a Literacy Instructional Tool in the Developmental Reading and Writing Classroom*. 2023, Texas Tech University, PhD Disseration.

Postman, Neil. *Amusing Ourselves to Death: Public Discourse in the Age of Show Business*. Penguin Books, 1986.

_____ and Charles Weingartner. *Teaching as a Subversive Activity*. New York: Delta Books, 1969.

_____. *Technopoly: The Surrender of Culture to Technology*. Vintage Books, 1993.

Robinson, Sir Ken. "Do Schools Kill Creativity." TEDEx, 2006.

Rowsell, Jennifer and Maureen Marsh. "Rethinking literacy education in new times : Multimodality, multiliteracies & new literacies." Brock Education: *A Journal of Educational Research and Practice*. Vol. 21(1), 2011, 53 - 62.

Ruspoli, Tao. *Being in the World. Documentary on the philosophy of Martin Heidegger*, 2010.

Sacks, Oliver. "The Machine Stops." *The Atlantic*, Feb. 14, 2019.

Serdyukov, P. "A Growing Formulization of Contemporary Online Education." *Academia Letters*, Article 2601, 2021.

Shah, Namank. "A Blurry Vision: Reconsidering the Failure of the One Laptop Per Child Initiative." Boston University Arts & Sciences Writing Program, 2011.

Shor, Ira. "What Is Critical Literacy?" *Journal of Pedagogy, Pluralism and Practice*, Volume 1(4), 1999.

Slouka, Mark. *War of the Worlds: Cyberspace and the High-Tech Assault on Reality*. Harper Collins Basic Books, 1995.

Skrbina, David. *The Metaphysics of Technology*. Routledge, 2014.

_____ . *Confronting Technology: Selected Readings and Essays*. Creative Fire Press, 2020.

Slouka, Mark (1996). *War of the Worlds: Cyberspace and the High-tech Assault on Reality*.

Small, Gary and Gigi Vorgan. *IBrain: Surviving the Technological Alteration of the Modern Mind*. Harper, 2009.

Smuckler, Elaine. "Why We Should Invite Our Demons to Tea." Blogpost, 2019.

Strauss, Valerie. "Why a leading professor of new media just banned technology use in class." *The Washington Post*, September 25, 2014.

Tapscott, Don. *Grown Up Digital: How the Net Generation is Changing Your World*. McGraw-Hill, 2008.

Toyama, Kentaro. "Why Technology Will Never Fix Education." *The Chronicle of Higher Education*, May 19, 2015.

Turkle, Sherry. *Alone Together: Why We Expect More from Technology and Less from Each Other*. Basic Books, 2011.

Twenge, Jean. *IGen: Why Today's Super-Connected Kids Are Growing Up Less Rebellious, More Tolerant, Less Happy—and Completely Unprepared for Adulthood—and What That Means for the Rest of Us*. Atria Books, 2017.

Young, Jeffrey. "What Happened to the $100 Laptop?" *EdSurge* Podcast, Nov. 5, 2019.

Zhong, Eddy. "School Makes Kids Less Intelligent." TEDxYouth, 2015.

Printed in the United States
by Baker & Taylor Publisher Services